JAMES GUNN 4

Blood Brand

Blood Brand

A JAMES GUNN Novel
by
John Delaney

MEWS BOOKS
LONDON AND CONNECTICUT

A Mews Original Publication
© Mews Books Limited 1977

*

FIRST MEWS PAPERBACK EDITION JANUARY 1977

*

Mews Books are published by
Mews Books Limited, 20 Bluewater Hill, Westport, Connecticut 06880
and distributed by
New English Library Limited, Barnard's Inn, Holborn, London EC1N 2JR
Made and printed in Great Britain by Hunt Barnard Printing Ltd., Aylesbury, Bucks.

45200062 9

Chapter One

There was trouble in the air, and James Gunn knew it. He recognised the smell of it, the delicate vibrations of tension in the air. The strange quietness which invariably preceded the eruption of violence. Only too well, Gunn recognised all the familiar signs. He had learned to live with trouble, even though he still could not get used to it.

Trouble did not ride with Gunn, nor did it follow him. It rode ahead, to await him wherever he travelled, an advance ambush or a predestined challenge. Things had been that way ever since Pine Fork.* Since he had taken on the Wendle Parker gang – one of the deadliest and most hated outlaw gangs ever to terrorise the Old West. Gunn had taken them on – and became a living legend by beating them. From the moment Wendle Parker had died under the blistering fire of Gunn's twin Colts, their owner had a reputation as a gunman to live with, live up to ... and kill for.

Since Pine Fork, there had been a dozen small towns, and a dozen challenges. In every town, every saloon, there was always a professional gunslinger, a drunk fired with too much Dutch courage, or a hot-headed kid in search of gun glory. The strange folk-lore of the West made things that way, perpetuated the endless chain of killings, for the man who shot down James Gunn automatically inherited his reputation and his legend. He became, in one simple squeeze of a trigger, the top gun, The Man.

*See *James Gunn 3: Hard Bounty*.

It was a tempting prize for those who sought to become legends. In a tough country where work was hard and rewards could be small, glory was a very special kind of currency.

A dozen towns, a dozen challenges. From those, eight gunfights and five dead men. When Gunn could back down with pride, or bluff it out until his challenger cooled off or lost his nerve, then he would do so. It didn't happen often. Faced with the almost inevitable shoot-out, Gunn would try to disarm his opponent, or avoid a fatal wound. It wasn't easy The five dead men testified to that.

Now Sagebrush Flats, Southern California, looked like becoming unlucky thirteen. It had looked that way from the moment Gunn had ridden in.

First the buzz of conversation as he was recognised. Gunn's striking appearance was an instrumental and unhelpful factor in spreading his fame. A tall, muscular man with a wild mane of long blond hair and ice-blue eyes might just go unnoticed in a crowd. But when he rode high in a hand-tooled English saddle, spoke with the clipped tones of an English gentleman and wore fringed buckskin clothing, he could not be a stranger for long in any new town.

Following closely upon recognition came the whispered rumours and wildly exaggerated stories. Dished up, added to, enhanced, they passed from mouth to ear, gaining something extra in each new exchange. Then came the speculation, the idle gossip. Was he really as fast as word had it? Could he be beaten? Was there a man in town who would have a chance against him?

There usually was such a man. The conversation would take a new and more dangerous turn then. More direct, more specific. Mere speculation became serious discussion, and eventually a fixed plan. The man, whoever he was, would find himself steered, inexorably, towards a showdown. His ego either boosted by flattery, or incited by mocking taunts, he would find himself set up as the next challenger. From that point onwards, the gunfight was no longer in any doubt. Only the exact time and place remained to be set.

In Sagebrush Flats, that man was Sam Lake. No longer young, he had tasted the bitter pleasures of being a fast gun just a few times too many. Now he was past his prime, and the edge had been taken off his speed. That rankled. No man likes his one quality, no matter how dubious, being taken away from him by the eroding finger of time. It made Lake vulnerable to the taunts and sly aspersions. Gunn's own youth, good looks and obvious virility gave him a seed of envy on which to build and nurture a hate. The people of Sagebrush Flats played upon Lake's weakness to placate their own vicarious need for thrills. They put the gun in his hand and primed the hammer. Then, satisfied, they could sit back and watch him pull the trigger.

He stood now at the bar of the Wild Deuce Saloon. Next to James Gunn. Close.

Too close. Gunn felt the man's elbow touch against his own, just enough to nudge him as he lifted his beer glass to his lips, spilling the liquor over the brim and down his fingers.

Gunn tried the easiest way out. Pretend it had been an accident, choose to ignore the opening move. He shifted his weight almost unnoticeably from one foot to the other, inching further down the bar and breaking physical contact. It should have been enough, but it wasn't.

'Kinda unsociable, ain't you, mister?' Lake glared sideways at him. 'You figger you're too good to drink alongside me?'

The direct jibe was too heavy to be ignored. Gunn pivoted slowly on his toes, facing Lake squarely. 'No offence intended, stranger,' he murmured in a soft, quiet voice. He forced a faint smile.

Lake was not appeased. Wrongly, he took Gunn's actions for a sign of weakness, and decided to push his luck. 'You'll have a drink with me, then?'

Gunn glanced down at his half-empty glass and shrugged gently. 'Sure, I'll have a drink with you.

Obliged.' He lifted the glass to his lips, draining it in one gulp.

Lake leaned across the bar and summoned the bartender. 'Gimme a glass of sarsaparilla for my friend here, will you?'

The barman looked nervous and worried. He approached Lake slowly, with caution. Elsewhere in the saloon, this last obvious insult had left the other customers in no doubt that a fight was imminent. They began to move, slowly, out of the line of fire, but in a position where they would be able to see the gunplay. A low murmur of voices broke out as someone started giving odds and taking bets upon the outcome.

Gunn himself watched the glass of sparkling soft beverage being placed in front of him and sighed heavily. He could not go on taking insults for much longer. He turned to Lake, his blue eyes blazing with a cold fire. 'I think you made a mistake, friend. I was drinking beer.'

It was his last attempt to cool things down. All Lake had to do was back off, treat it as a joke. He didn't.

'Ain't no mistake. I buy the drinks, I call the shots. You gonna insult me by refusing?'

Gunn looked down at the sarsaparilla for a second, then glanced back up at Lake and nodded slowly. 'Yes my friend, I'm very much afraid that I am,' he said calmly.

Lake pushed himself away from the bar, his eyes narrowed to slits. 'I paid good money for that drink. I suggest you drink it. Sure hate to see money wasted.'

Gunn nodded. 'So do I. How's about drinking it yourself?'

The tension was at breaking point. The two men stood, facing each other in cold rage. Suddenly, a tall figure stepped between them. He tossed a quarter carelessly on to the top of the bar, turning to Lake. 'Looks like you two gentlemen got a small problem,' he muttered in an easy voice. 'Be glad to help you out by paying for that drink you don't want. Ain't nothing I like better'n a nice cool glass of sarsaparilla on a hot day.'

His hand reached out for the glass on the counter. Both Gunn's and Lake's eyes were on it just as the stranger had intended. Thus distracted, neither saw the stranger's other hand snaking towards his gunbelt.

The man stepped back a couple of paces as the Walker-Colt leapt into his hand. He eyed Lake and Gunn cooly. 'Seems to me you two fellers were about to get into a whole lot of bother over a damn fool drink,' he observed. 'Don't like to see men getting 'emselves killed over nothing.'

Gunn stared into the stranger's eyes. They held the merest hint of a twinkle, belying the years which showed on his weather-beaten face. 'You're more than welcome to that drink, stranger,' he murmured politely.

Lake was not so affable. His face was black with impotent rage. 'You got no call to interfere, Cunningham,' he spat out.

Cunningham turned on him, a certain degree of apology in his face. 'Looks like I'm gonna have to prove a point, Sam,' he said. 'Both of you, please lift out one of your guns real easy, and lay 'em on the counter.' The Walker-Colt jerked slightly in his hand to back up the request. Sullenly, Lake obeyed. Gunn lifted his own right-hand Colt very gingerly by the extreme end of its ivory butt and laid it alongside Lake's weapon.

'OK. Now crack open the chambers and take your slugs out,' Cunningham went on. He waited for Gunn and Lake to comply before speaking again. 'Now, the way I see it, you two fellers were just about on the verge of having a gunfight,' he said quietly. 'Only point proved by that is that one of you would prove to be faster than the other. Only trouble is, one of you gets to be dead.' He nodded down at the unloaded, harmless guns on the counter. 'All right, pick 'em up and put 'em back.'

Gunn and Lake did as they were told. Quite apart from the Walker-Colt in his hand, Cunningham had an air of quiet authority about him. He was obviously a man used to have others obeying his commands. Feeling safe now that there was to be no lead flying, the other occupants of the saloon clustered around the bar to get a close-up view of the situation Cunningham had so neatly taken charge of.

'OK. Now you can have your gunfight,' Cunningham announced. 'When I call "draw" we'll see which of you can pull iron and fire first. And nobody dies of lead poisoning.'

Gunn entered fully into the spirit of the thing, now that the imminent danger had been reduced to little more than a harmless game. He pushed himself away from the bar and dropped back a couple of paces, facing Sam Lake squarely.

'Draw' called Cunningham softly.

Gunn's hand moved in a blur of speed down to the ivory butt of his Colt. The gun slipped free of leather in one smooth, continuous movement, the barrel coming up into line with Sam Lake's stomach a good three-fifths of a second before the man had freed his own gun from his holster. The faint click of Gunn's hammer slamming down on an empty chamber sounded uncannily loud in the hushed atmosphere of the saloon, and seemed to have just as great a psychological effect as a real gunshot would have had. Sam Lake's face paled instantly, and a look of fear crossed his eyes as he realised how near to death he had been. A low murmur of wonder rippled round the saloon.

Cunningham nodded knowingly, and turned to the shaken Lake. 'Now you tell me I had no call to interfere, Sam,' he murmured pointedly.

The man made no reply. Instead, a faint shudder seemed to ripple through his whole body. Whirling on his heel, he stamped out of the saloon, just as the first nervous titters of laughter began to break out.

'I'm much obliged to you,' Gunn said quietly.

Cunningham smiled openly now, knowing the immediate danger was past. 'Like I said, mister, I don't hold with folks killing each other over stupid things.'

'You're a brave man,' Gunn complimented him. 'Doing what you did took a lot of guts.'

Cunningham shrugged almost carelessly. 'Hell, I know Sam Lake too well,' he said. 'He ain't a bad man, all told. Sam's trouble is, he's living in his own past and he just can't get used to the notion of growing old gracefully. I guess we just taught him an important lesson in life, between the two of us.'

Gunn ignored the man's modesty. 'You might have known Sam Lake, but you didn't know me,' he pointed out. 'For all you knew, I could have been a killer, with a real mean streak.'

Cunningham laughed softly. 'Oh, I know you, Mister Gunn. Or rather, I know of you, and I guess that's the next best thing.'

Gunn was puzzled. 'I don't understand?'

'A real good friend of mine, over in Silver Creek, Utah,' Cunningham explained. 'Big Dan Emmerson . . . you helped him out some, a while back.*

'Dan?' Gunn was overjoyed to hear of his old friend again. 'Hell, he's a good man. A good friend to have. He paused for a second, grinning somewhat ruefully. 'But you're wrong about me helping him out. It was more the other way round.'

Cunningham shrugged, signifying that there was little difference between the two. 'Anyways, Dan wrote me a lot about you,' he went on. 'But even if you were a complete stranger, I saw the way you tried to back down from that gunfight, even at high cost to your pride, Mister Gunn. Takes a special kind of man to do that. A man worth stepping in for and helping.'

'I'm glad you did,' Gunn assured him once again. 'Truth to tell, it makes me sick to my stomach to have to stay on this killing trail.' As he spoke, he slid his twin Colts from their holsters slowly, laying them upon the bar-top and studying the message engraved on each shiny barrel. The inscription was terse, but carried a depth of meaning: 'Never in Anger'.

Cunningham saw the words, too, and nodded under-

*See *James Gunn 2: Silver for a Bullet.*

11

standingly. 'Takes some living up to, sometimes, don't it?'

Gunn left the Colts on the counter, lapsing into thoughtful silence. It was Cunningham who spoke first. 'Looks to me like you could do with staying well clear of towns for a spell, Gunn.'

Gunn smiled wistfully. 'I wish I could,' he admitted.

'Reckon I could help you out, maybe,' Cunningham suggested tentatively. 'That's if you're looking for a job, of course.'

Gunn was immediately interested, but past experiences had taught him to be cautious. 'Could well be,' he said guardedly. 'What's your business, Mr Cunningham?'

'Horses,' Cunningham said simply. 'You know much about horses, Mr Gunn?'

'Some,' Gunn muttered modestly.

Cunningham nodded. 'Kinda figgered you might,' he murmured. 'Noticed you ride an English saddle. Anyone can use a rig like that in a country like this has just got to be a pretty good horseman.'

'Or a fool?' Gunn challenged, half-jokingly.

Cunningham smiled easily. 'Any man can tell you're not that, Mr Gunn.'

'Jim.' Gunn held out his hand in friendship. 'Go ahead, I'm interested.'

Cunningham accepted the handshake. 'Name's John,' he said. 'Real pleased to meet you. Fact is, I breed horses. Could do with a good man around the place, sort of a general hand. You'd have your own quarters, eat with me and the missus, and a hundred and twenty dollars a month on top. Grab you?'

Gunn didn't really need to think about it. Horses were his first love. If things had gone differently, he would have started his life in the New World doing exactly the same as John Cunningham.* That dream was gone, for the present. Maybe the next best thing would be to work for Cunningham. He presented his hand again, to clinch

*See *James Gunn 1: The Deadly Stranger*.

the agreement. 'You got yourself a deal,' he said, gratefully.

'Good,' Cunningham said. 'Anytime you're ready, we can ride out to the ranch. It's a good ten miles outside town. Should suit you down to the ground.'

'Right,' Gunn agreed, thinking of the inner peace he would gain from the simple act of just hanging up his Colts on a wall and forgetting about them for a while. 'If it's all right with you, we'll just have a drink to celebrate, then we'll be on our way.'

Cunningham clapped him on the back, laughing. 'Damn good idea, Jim. Sure was dreading the thought of picking up that sarsaparilla.'

The two men laughed together, relaxing in the bonds of newly-formed friendship. Gunn ordered two beers and held up his glass in toast. 'To your health.'

They drank quietly for several minutes. Glancing down to the bar, Gunn saw his two Colts laying there harmlessly, and smiled to himself. It looked like a good omen for the future.

Chapter Two

The weeks passed quickly and quietly at the Circle 8
ranch. There was plenty to do, for Cunningham only
kept one other ranch hand. In the past, he had been
content to do 90 per cent of the work himself. Gunn's
presence gave him a chance to apply himself to other
things. Much of Cunningham's business was in breeding
good solid work horses for freight-pulling, the sure-
footed and strong little quarter-horse, and ponies for
sale to the youngsters from the surrounding area. But
Cunningham had dreams of better things. Now, with
Gunn's help, he stood a chance of doing something
about those dreams. He spent more and more time tour-
ing the horse auctions, buying new stock and taking
orders for his own business.

For his own part, Gunn was more than happy to be
left in charge. He immersed himself in sheer hard work,
and felt all the better for it. The days were long, Gunn
rising at sun-up and rarely bunking down until it was
well past dusk. Cunningham could not help but note
the enthusiasm with which Gunn threw himself into his
chores, and the bond of friendship and respect between
the two men deepened more and more.

It was mid-afternoon when Cunningham returned from
one of his buying expeditions. Proudly, he led a pair of
jet-black mares into the corral where Gunn was working.

'What do you think, Jim? Real beauties, ain't they?'

Gunn looked at the two horses with undisguised
admiration – almost reverence. They were indeed

beauties. Gunn's keen eye for horseflesh could find no fault with the pair of animals. From their sleek, glossy coats down to the fine set of their trim fetlocks, the horses were thoroughbreds, through and through.

Gunn whistled through his teeth. 'They're fine, John, just fine,' he murmured. A slightly quizzical frown creased his brow. 'But they're thoroughbreds . . . not your usual run of stock. You got something special in mind?'

Cunningham laughed happily. 'You don't miss a trick, Jim. Yep, I got something special in mind, all right. Something I've dreamed about for more years than I care to remember.'

Cunningham crossed the corral to where a small fire blazed in a brick-built furnace. Picking up his branding irons, he thrust them into the flames. Returning to Gunn, he clicked his teeth with irritation. 'A pair of horses as beautiful as that . . . seems a real crime to disfigure 'em with a brand, don't it?' Without waiting for a reply, he went on: 'Still, it has to be done. Can't take chances out here, especially with real good bloodstock like this.'

Gunn nodded by way of reply. Since coming to America, he had often reflected upon the seeming brutality of hot-iron branding. At home in England, such a thing was unnecessary and quite unthinkable. Out in the West, where cattle and horse-thieving was commonplace, it was a different matter.

He tethered the first horse against the fence, taking a rope up around its proud neck to hold it steady whilst Cunningham burned his mark into the animal's hide.

'I'll do it down under the belly – where it don't show too much,' Cunningham muttered as he returned with the glowing branding iron. He knelt below the horse, jabbing the searing iron into its belly.

The horse let out a shrill whinny of agony, bucking and rearing to escape the torture. It took all Gunn's considerable strength to keep the animal from breaking free and bolting. He turned his head away as the stench

15

of singed hair and flesh curled up to his nostrils.

At last it was done. Cunningham pulled the branding iron away. There for the horse's natural life, was the mark of ownership deeply carved in its flesh. The brand of the Circle 8 ranch – a figure of eight inside a larger zero.

'Never did ask you – why Circle 8?' Gunn asked, more to make conversation than any attempt to pry.

Cunningham looked up and smiled. 'That was how I started,' he explained. 'With just eight horses and no money. Kinda thought it was appropriate at the time.'

Gunn looked up to glance around the huge spread, and the hundreds of horses. 'You've come a long way,' he said without envy.

'Yep, I guess so,' Cunningham said, nodding. 'But I got dreams, Jim – even now. These two mares are the start of realising one of 'em.'

'You want to tell me about it.'

Cunningham nodded eagerly. 'You bet I do,' he said. 'Ain't no use having a dream if you can't share it with someone.' He returned to the fire and heated up the iron again. When he had branded the second horse, and rubbed a soothing ointment into both raw wounds, he led Gunn to the side of the corral and sat up on the top fence rail to light up a small black cheroot.

'Thing is, Jim, I've dreamed for years of breeding and raising another type of horse,' he started.

Gunn glanced at the two black mares. 'Racers?'

'Yeah, Jim – racehorses,' Cunningham murmured. His eyes had a dreamy, far-away look in them as he spoke. 'Over on the coast, Jim – places like San Francisco, Santa Anna – there's fortunes being made with racehorses. It's going to be one of the great sports of America one of these days, Jim, just you mark my words.'

Gunn smiled inwardly at the man's almost child-like enthusiasm, but he said nothing. He had already noticed that Cunningham's attitude was typical of the New World – the boundless, restless enthusiasm of a young nation, with big new ideas and the fervent belief that they were blazing new trails, pointing a new way for the rest of the world to follow. Gunn didn't have the heart to point out that horse racing had been a favourite sport of the English aristocracy for hundreds of years. Instead, he just nodded sagely. 'You're making a fine start,' he murmured, casting an appreciative sidelong glance at the two mares once again.

'They're only half of it,' Cunningham went on excitedly. 'The other, and most important part lies over the border, in Mexico. That's where you come in, Jim. I need your help.'

Gunn didn't understand. 'Mexico?'

Cunningham nodded. 'There's a Spanish nobleman, Don Santoz, just over the border in the San Orato Valley. He owns a whole string of almost legendary black stallions. They're derived from absolutely pure Arab bloodstock, the line going back for a couple of dozen generations. The finest horseflesh you'd ever hope to set eyes on – the seeds of a new breed which could be unbeatable, Jim.'

Gunn saw the blaze of ambitious excitement dancing in Cunningham's eyes. 'So where do I come in?' he wanted to know.

'I want you to go down there,' Cunningham told him. 'I want you to go and see Don Santoz. Try to buy a couple of those stallions, or even just arrange some form of breeding arrangement on my behalf.'

'Why don't you go yourself?'

Cunningham grinned ruefully. 'You'd stand a better chance,' he muttered. 'Like I said, Don Santoz is a nobleman – of the old school. I'm just a jumped-up dirt farmer. He would see me as someone beneath his dignity. You're a gentleman, Jim, you got breeding in your lineage. Quite apart from which, you're English.'

'What's that got to do with it?' Gunn queried.

Cunningham let out a short, somewhat bitter laugh. 'A helluva lot,' he answered flatly. 'There's plenty of folks – both sides of the border – who don't want to forget the Alamo.' He paused, his face serious. 'I don't want to mislead you, Jim. It might not be an easy trip.'

Gunn purposely evaded the warning. He could see just how much the trip meant to his friend. He made his mind up in an instant. 'When do you want me to go?' he asked smiling.

Cunningham beamed, clapping him on the back. 'Anytime you're ready,' he retorted joyfully. 'The sooner the better, as far as I'm concerned. Those mares will be coming into season pretty soon.'

Gunn pondered for a moment about the immediate workload on the Circle 8. 'Reckon you can handle things here on your own for a couple of weeks?'

Cunningham dismissed the query with a casual wave of his hand. 'Heck, I always managed well enough in the past. Reckon two weeks of hard work again ain't gonna kill me.'

It appeared to be settled. Gunn nodded thoughtfully. 'Well, in that case, there's nothing stopping me setting out almost at once,' he said. 'Tomorrow, maybe.'

'Great.' Cunningham slipped his arm around Gunn's shoulders. 'Come on, let's go into the house and eat. I'll have Lydia rustle up something special – sort of a celebration dinner. You'll need something sustaining inside you if you're gonna tackle that ride in the morning. It's a rough ride down into the San Orato Valley, and that desert sun can get darn hot.'

They walked back to the ranch-house, discussing the final details.

'You think I should get an early night and make a start at sun-up?' Gunn asked.

Cunningham shook his head. 'Nope, if you're wise, you won't leave until just after noon,' he said. 'Like I said, that sun gets mighty hot. It's best to travel in the afternoon, when it gets a mite cooler.'

That suited Gunn just fine. The extra few hours in the morning would give him time to drop into town, have a shave and a haircut and buy some new clothes. He wanted to make the best possible impression on Don

18

Santoz, for Cunningham's sake.

Lydia Cunningham greeted the two men with a querulous smile. She knew her husband well enough to tell when something was in the air. She too was happy when she heard the news. She cuddled her husband lovingly, smiling up at Gunn. 'It's good you came here, Jim,' she said warmly. 'And it's good you're doing this for John. God knows, he's worked hard enough for long enough. It's about time he achieved some of his dreams. A good man deserves a little reward out of life.'

'I just hope I can pull it off,' Gunn murmured.

Lydia Cunningham bent over him and planted a chaste peck on the side of his face. 'You'll do just fine, Jim. I know you will.'

She hastened off to prepare a meal. Gunn and Cunningham sat smoking cigars and talking of horses. There didn't seem to be any problems. It all seemed easy.

Perhaps too easy!

Chapter Three

Gunn plucked his gunbelt down from the nail on the wall and buckled it on once again with mixed feelings. It had felt good to walk without it in the past few weeks. Good not to have to carry the weight of the twin Colts, with their constant reminder of the violence which haunted his past and clouded his future.

Yet Gunn had to be a realist. The Colt was the instrument of order in this wild country. Where no man dared to stand up and speak for human rights, the gun spoke rough justice and a kind of law. It also stood for simple survival. Out in the desert, where Gunn was headed, death waited in many forms. The rattlesnake, the coyote, the mountain lion – they were only some of the dangers which also shrank only before the power of the gun. There were others: rogue Indians, outlaws, Mexican bandits once he crossed the border.

All this, Gunn rationalised to himself as he checked each Colt in turn, spinning the chambers, cocking the hammers and easing them back again, spinning them in his hand to readjust himself to the balance and feel of the weapons before slipping them neatly and snugly back into their leather holsters.

He walked out of the bunk-house and stared up into the sky, shielding his eyes from the harsh glare of the overhead sun. It was almost at it's zenith now, throwing down the waves of incredible, searing heat that could cook a man alive from the inside. Cunningham had been right. Noon was no time to venture into the Mexican desert.

Gunn saddled up, making sure that the open bank draft Cunningham had entrusted him with was in a safe place, tucked well away in his saddlebags. He made a last check on all his equipment for the trip – water flasks, food supplies, blankets and armaments. Beside his Springfield rifle, Gunn had tucked a squat, short-barrelled scattergun into an improvised rope holster. Its extra weight was more than justified, for at short range, a shotgun could be a far more effective weapon than any hand gun when it came to dealing with poison-ous snakes. And they were one thing the Mexican desert abounded with. Snakes, scorpions, the brightly coloured Gila lizard and the deadly Tarantula spider – every kind of life that could slither or crawl put Man in his place in the desert, showing him plainly that he was not in his natural element, that he was a frail creature, despite his intelligence.

Satisfied at last, Gunn swung himself up into the saddle without using the stirrups. He gathered in the reins and glanced back at the porch of the ranch-house, where Lydia and John Cunningham stood together, waving him goodbye. Gunn raised one arm high in the air, then dropped both hands to the reins and spurred his mount into motion.

He rode towards Sagebrush Flats at a leisurely pace, not wishing to tire his horse unduly before tackling rougher country. Riding into town, he tethered the beast outside the general store and sauntered in. He bought a couple of shirts and a crisp white linen jacket, with a matching pair of lightweight trousers. 'Wrap them up for me, will you?' Gunn asked the storekeeper as he paid for the goods. 'I'm just going over to the barber shop for a freshen up.'

The storekeeper nodded, ringing up the sale. He watched his customer walk out of the door and down the street. Only when he saw Gunn enter the barber shop did he tear off his apron, lock the front door and hurry to the rear exit. He had a message to deliver.

Gunn sat in the barber's chair and relaxed. 'Could do with a bit of a trim and a nice close shave,' he murmured.

The barber nodded, wrapping a clean white towel around Gunn's neck and shoulders. He set about trimming Gunn's long, golden locks.

'Not too much, you understand?' Gunn told him. 'If I wanted to get scalped, I'd find myself an Indian barber.'

'You wanna talk some?' asked the barber.

'Nope.' Gunn settled down even more comfortably in the chair. The haircut progressed in peaceful silence.

Afterwards, his face swathed in hot towels, Gunn watched patiently as the barber whipped up a creamy shaving foam and stropped his gleaming razor on a leather strap. He pumped up the chair to a more convenient height. He was just about to bend over Gunn and start work when he froze, his eyes riveted.

Gunn heard the faint click of the front door opening behind him and warning bells sounded faintly inside his head. He peered over the frozen barber's shoulder into the mirror behind him.

The door had been thrown wide open. There, framed in the portal, stood Sam Lake, his Colt already in his hand. Just behind him, two mean-looking youngsters lurked, evil grins twisting on their faces.

Gunn stiffened, instinctively, in the chair.

'Freeze,' Lake's harsh voice barked out. The Colt trembled in his hand. He stepped forward smartly, coming round in front of the chair where Gunn sat, helpless.

Lake glanced up at the frightened barber with a look of contempt. 'Ain't you got something to tend to out back?'

For a second, the barber's face looked puzzled. 'No, there ain't nothing I got to do,' he started to say. Then comprehension dawned. His face paled even more. Stammering awkwardly, he backed to the rear door. I'll just go attend some chores.'

He disappeared, closing and locking the door behind

him. Lake stood over Gunn, his finger tightly curled around the trigger of his Colt. There was a wicked grin twisting up the corners of his mouth. 'Ain't got Cunningham to help you today, eh Mister Gunn?' he observed.

Gunn nodded his head sideways at Lake's two side-kicks. 'See you couldn't manage without a little help yourself,' he muttered pointedly.

For a second, the smile faded from Lake's face, to be replaced by a vicious scowl. Then his eyes fell upon the gleaming blade of the cut-throat razor the barber had abandoned, and then the terrible grin returned. He reached out carefully, picking the razor up in his left hand. He looked down at the fine edge thoughtfully. 'Well, lookee here. Just all sharpened up and ready to give you a nice, close shave, Gunn,' he hissed. 'Maybe the closest darned shave you ever had in your life.'

Behind him, Lake's two cohorts giggled nastily. 'Didn't know you was a barber, Sam,' one of them called.

Lake shrugged carelessly, playing on the sick joke. 'Well, let's just say I'm still in training,' he muttered. 'I still need a whole lot of practice. Mister Gunn here looks just like the sort of feller who'd give me a chance to improve myself.' He gave another nasty little laugh. 'Yes sir, I'd say Mister Gunn here was just cut out for the job.'

He leaned forward, swinging the evil blade gently from side to side. The back of the razor just brushed across Gunn's throat. Lake called to his two companions. 'Could use a little help here. Need one of you to come and lather Mister Gunn up, real nice.'

One of the young gunslingers stepped forward, sheathing his Trantor in its holster. He picked up the abandoned shaving brush and holder, stirring up the lather once again. With crude careless strokes, he slapped the foam across Gunn's face, managing to push the bristles of the brush up Gunn's nose and into his mouth.

Gunn fought to control the cold rage surging inside him. He had to stay cool if he was to stand a chance against the three men. Turning his head slightly to one side, he spat out the bitter-tasting soap on to the floor and returned his gaze to Lake.

'Better just check this razor's sharp enough,' the man muttered, as he spoke, he flashed the blade down in front of Gunn's face, missing his nose by no more than a hair's breadth. Continuing on its downward path, the keen blade neatly sliced the top button off Gunn's shirt. 'Yep, looks fine to me,' Lake observed. He brought his hand up slowly, holding the razor on a level with Gunn's eyes.

Gunn's body tensioned like a fine spring. Some sixth inner sense told him that the fooling was over. There was a chilling look of vicious hate on Lake's face.

The man moved, in a blur of speed. His arm lashed down and sideways, the blade slicing in an arc which would take it deep into Gunn's cheek. The move was fast, but Gunn was faster. He threw his head on to one side as the razor flashed harmlessly through the air with a horrible swishing sound. At the same time, Gunn's foot stabbed down on the chair's pump-pedal which he had quietly and secretly located seconds earlier. With a faint hiss, the raised chair sank to its normal level.

Too late, Lake saw the danger and his finger tightened on the trigger of the Colt in his hand. The slug whistled harmlessly over Gunn's head as he reached for his own weapon and slid it smoothly from its holster. Gunn kicked out at the floor, spinning the swivel chair as the Colt came up into position. Fanning the hammer with the ball of his left palm, Gunn emptied all six chambers, spewing a death-dealing arc of flying lead all around the interior of the small barber's shop.

Lake staggered backwards, slammed into the mirror on the wall by the impact of Gunn's first two bullets. The glass splintered and smashed, showering to the floor together with broken bottles of hair tonic and skin lotions. For a few seconds, Lake remained standing, propped up by the wall. Then his legs slid away from underneath him in the gooey mess on the floor. He slid, slowly down the wall, making horrible noises in his throat. Gunn's first bullet had taken him high in the chest, smashing and splintering his collarbone before deflecting upwards to tear out most of his thorax. A severed artery spurted crimson to mingle with the coloured lotions on the floor. He died, slowly and horribly, choking in his own blood.

The barber's chair was still spinning slowly as Gunn leapt out of it to check on the rest of his gunplay. One of Lake's young and hotheaded companions had paid the full and terrible price of falling into bad company. Two slugs had seared into his stomach, just below the ribcage. He was not quite dead, but the remainder of his life was being counted off in seconds.

The third gunman had been luckier. A stray bullet had merely creased the side of his head, gouging out an angry red groove of torn flesh but leaving his skull intact. He lay slumped on the floor, unconscious. He was lucky indeed. He would stand up again – with little more than a headache for a few hours and a scar for life.

Gunn sighed heavily to himself, reviewing the carnage. The few, brief weeks of peace had been too good to last. Reflecting bitterly upon the seemingly fixed pattern of his life, Gunn blew gently down the barrel of his Colt to cool it, snapped open the chamber and slid in six fresh cartridges before jabbing it back into its holster. Then, stooping to the floor, he picked up the razor laying by Lake's body and moved to the one small and jagged section of mirror still fixed to the wall. With half a dozen swift, sure strokes, he shaved himself and wiped his face on a clean towel.

He turned to leave. On an afterthought, he delved into his pocket and brought out a dime. Casually, he tossed it on to the barber's chair and headed for the door.

Opening it, Gunn looked out into the street. Just as he had expected, the sounds of shooting had attracted an expectant crowd. A gasp of surprise went up as they saw who was framed in the shop doorway. James Gunn was the last person on Earth any of the townsfolk had expected to see walk out of that doorway.

Gunn propped himself against the door, waiting. It didn't take long. The sheriff, accompanied by the white-coated figure of the little barber, hastened along the street towards him.

Sheriff Baines held his shotgun lazily in one hand, the butt tucked under his armpit. He stepped straight past Gunn, peering into the interior of the shop. Ducking his head out again, he sucked at his teeth pensively as he looked up at Gunn's emotionless face. 'Dead?'

'Two of them,' Gunn retorted. 'The other one's just suffering from a .45 calibre hair parting.'

Baines nodded. 'Fancy shootin',' he observed, the faintest trace of awe in his voice. 'Folks bin wondering for weeks if Sam Lake could take you. Now they know, I guess.'

'And the other two?'

'Jess and Conrad Shobrook. Conrad's the one with the holes in him. There's two more brothers in the clan. They ain't gonna take kindly to you slicing off a quarter of the family.'

'They were hell-bent on slicing a good part of me off,' Gunn pointed out, icily. 'Didn't give me a great deal of choice.'

The sheriff nodded understandingly, inclining his head towards the little barber. 'Yep, I know. Phil here told me how it happened. Ain't got no case against you, Gunn.'

'That mean I'm free to go?' Gunn asked.

'Yep,' Baines replied.

Gunn stepped off the boardwalk into the street, pre-paring to cross to the general store and pick up his purchases.

'Gunn?' Baines called softly after him.

Gunn turned round. 'Yes, sheriff?'

'Kinda be obliged if you'd stay outta town.'

Gunn smiled grimly. 'Exactly what I had in mind, sheriff.' He turned away and walked down the dusty street towards the store. The storekeeper waited for him in the doorway, a neatly-wrapped package in his hands.

He thrust it out at arms length as though it were a bundle of fused dynamite.

'Obliged,' Gunn murmured, accepting the package. He walked to his horse, stuffed the new clothes into his saddlebag and mounted up. Every pair of eyes in town followed him as he left at a fast trot.

Hardly had his mount's hoof-beats faded into the distance than the sound of two more approaching horses echoed down the main street of Sagebrush Flats. Two riders, their faces grim, galloped through the crowd and dismounted in front of the barber shop. They walked in, as a buzz of conversation wafted all around them.

Inside the shop, Brendan and Wesley Shobrook looked down on the blood-spattered body of their brother. Seeing that he was past any help, they turned their attention to Jess, who was just regaining consciousness. They bent over him, helping him to his feet.

All three brothers turned to look once more at their dead sibling. There was a hushed silence. Finally, Wesley, the oldest of the brothers spoke in a quiet, menacing hiss. 'We'll fix that sonovabitch. I swear on your life, Conrad, we'll fix him real good.'

Together, they turned and pushed back past the sheriff and through the crowd. Baines let them go, saying nothing. It was out of his hands. It was family matter. In the West, that went above and beyond the law. Revenge, however unjustified, was understandable, and therefore excuseable. The law was not enough. Blood had to pay for blood. That was the way things were.

Chapter Four

Four hours of hard and uncompromising riding took Gunn over the border between the North and the South. This was no-man's land – a vast tract of inhospitable desert that neither side wanted. There remained over thirty miles of desert before Gunn would come to the nearest Mexican village, and the Santoz hacienda lay another ten miles beyond that.

As the sun crept lower in the sky, Gunn started to keep his eyes peeled for a suitable campsite for the night. He had no wish to bed down on the desert floor, for at night a bitter cold rushed in to take the place of the searing heat of the day, and any creature at ground level was fair prey for the fanged denizens of the desert who hunted without light, needing only their sense of smell and their sensitivity to bodyheat to find a kill.

On the distant horizon, Gunn could see an irregular mound of volcanic rocks, spewed out of the desert floor countless centuries before, when the arid sands had been a lush tropical paradise. Gunn's keen eyes estimated the distance, converting it into travelling time. Shielding his eyes with his hand, he stared into the setting sun, gauging what remained of its height above the horizon.

There was time to spare. It would not be dark for a good hour. Gunn slowed his horse, allowing the tired beast to derive some benefit from the rapidly cooling atmosphere.

He reached the outcrop of rocks just as the last glowing segment of the sun was slipping out of sight. In the fading light, Gunn found himself a sheltered place, scoured away the loose stones from the shale and dusty soil and spread out his bed-roll. There was nothing around to use for kindling wood and fuel, Gunn contented himself with an evening meal of sourdough bread and some cold, cooked beans. The simple repast over, Gunn propped himself against a boulder and lit a small cheroot. It would be an early night.

Before nine, Gunn prepared to turn in. He took an oil-soaked torch from his saddlebag and lit it. In its flickering light, he examined the immediate area around his sleeping position carefully, not forgetting to peer into every nook and cranny between the surrounding rocks. Such places were natural haunting grounds of snakes and scorpions. Finding nothing, Gunn made his last preparations for the night and doused the torch. He fell asleep quickly, lulled by the absolute silence of the desert around him.

The still silence was broken. Though it was no more than the faintest crunch of boot upon gravel, it was enough to wake Gunn immediately. He pricked his ears, straining towards the source of the faint sound. His eyes peered into the darkness, broken only by the dim light of the halfmoon overhead.

In the gloom, three shadowy figures crept stealthily towards him. Gunn's body tensed beneath his blankets, his right hand creeping down to his side.

The group of three broke up. Two of the figures continued towards him, whilst the other crept over to his horse. Still feigning sleep, Gunn peered up through slitted eyes, taking full stock of his situation. He could just make out a dull blur of dark-skinned faces as the two men stood over him. Indians, perhaps, or more likely Mexican bandidos. One of them held a Colt in his hand, the other's fingers were firmly wrapped around the hilt of a Bowie knife. Its shiny blade glinted in the ghostly moonlight.

The man with the gun came closer, holding it out at arm's length, pointed at Gunn's head. There was the faintest click of the hammer being drawn back and cocked.

'Hey, gringo, wake up, heh?' the man hissed. At the same time, his boot shot out to jab Gunn in the side.

The blow never connected. Gunn was ready for it. He rolled to one side, his right arm coming up under the blanket with the shortened scattergun held ready. It discharged with a dull roar, the full sound being muffled by the thick blanket. The Mexican fell backwards, screaming in agony and clawing uselessly at the bloody jelly he had left for a face. He was dead before he hit the ground.

The second attacker was stunned for a split second. Time enough for Gunn to swing round the shotgun and let him have the full blast of the second barrel in the gut. He made no sound at all as the narrow cone of pellets blasted straight through and out of his back, taking a large section of his spinal column with them.

Rolling over twice more, Gunn ended up on his stomach with his hand around the butt of his right-hand Colt. It came free of leather as the third bandit started to run away from his horse. Two slugs chewed their way into his back, killing him before his legs stopped their automatic motion. Although dead, he covered several more yards before his body slumped forwards to lie face-down in the dust.

Gunn held his breath, listening intently and staring into the gloom. There was no sound and no sign of movement. After several minutes, Gunn scrambled to his feet. There had only been the three of them. He crossed to his horse and drew out the torch again. Lighting it, he examined each one of the bodies in turn. They were Mexican bandits all right. Each wore a crossed bandolier of ammunition across their chests, and their filthy, tattered clothes showed that they were denizens of the desert and the foothills.

Gunn shuddered as he looked down upon the two shattered shotgun victims. It was far from being a pretty sight. At close range, it was not only snakes who were

30

torn to shreds by the shrieking hail of pellets. The lead did just as much damage to two-legged reptiles.

Satisfied that there were no more bandits in the immediate vicinity, Gunn sat down to think. Commonsense told him that this sort of bandit gang invariably travelled in much larger numbers. This being so, the trio which had nearly bushwhacked him must be some kind of an advance scouting party. The rest would not be too far behind.

He dragged the three bodies under the largest overhanging rock, kicking dust over them in a vain attempt to soak up the crimson pool of blood. The scent of it would attract every coyote from miles around.

Thinking of this, and also of the dead bandits' companions, Gunn lifted his bedroll and threw it over his shoulder. Carefully, he climbed up the rocks until he was a good thirty feet above the ground. Finding a narrow ledge on a flat-topped boulder, he spread the roll out as best he could and lay down again. He was asleep again in minutes, secure in the knowledge that neither man nor beast could scramble up the slippery shale and rocks towards him without making noise to wake the dead.

Gunn awoke as the first rays of early morning sunlight began to pierce through the shadows between the rocks. He rose quickly, peering out across the desert for any signs of life. There were none.

He stooped over to roll up his bedding and buckled on his gunbelt. Some inner, sixth sense made him upend his boots and shake them out before slipping them on to his feet. It proved to be a wise precaution. A huge, black and hairy tarantula dropped quietly from its snug sleeping place and began to scuttle to the safety of the nearest dark crevice. Instinctively, filled with loathing, Gunn smashed the heel of the boot down upon the ugly creature, crushing it into a sticky, furry smear against the rocks. Shuddering with revulsion, Gunn turned away to lace his boots.

As Gunn saddled up, a ring of circling buzzards

gathered above his head. The birds, with their uncanny knack of tracking down dead and decaying flesh. had already picked out the three dead Mexicans for their morning meal. They waited only for the one live human to ride away and leave them to their feast.

Gunn thought, briefly, about burying his attackers, then forced the idea from his mind. After their sneak attempt to kill him, Gunn did not feel disposed towards depriving the buzzards of their banquet. Besides, the birds would serve as a useful marker for the remainder of the outlaw gang. Seeing the fate of their comrades might just serve to dissuade them from similar bushwhacking attempts in the future. He set his horse at a fast gallop, eager to make as much distance as possible before the sun reached its zenith and began punishing the desert with the intolerable midday heat again.

Two hours riding brought him to the small village of Salsarito. He trotted into the centre of the settlement warily, acutely aware of the suspicious eyes following him every step of the way. Cunningham had warned him that U.S. currency would be of little use to him over the border. As an emergency fund, Gunn had brought a small quantity of gold dust with him. It served to buy water for his horse, and a welcome meal of tortillas and chili beans for himself.

After eating, he indulged himself in the local custom of taking a siesta in a shady place until the midday heat had started to wane. He slept with one eye open, and a hand resting on his gunbelt. It was a sensible precaution.

A small Mexican boy gave him exact directions to the Santoz hacienda. It was no more than two hours ride, the child informed him, but the intervening space was bad land, filled with bandidos and renegade gringos on the run from the law and order the other side of the border. Gunn thanked the boy, rewarded him with a handful of rifle bullets – hard and valuable currency in a land where a dozen heads of corn could buy a life. The child scurried off, eager to exchange his new-found wealth for words of praise, or a day's rest from the harsh work in the dusty, arid fields.

Refreshed, both horse and rider made good time through the rough country, and the Santoz Ranch soon appeared in the distance – a safe and welcome oasis in the dangerous wilderness.

Or so it seemed, from a distance. Gunn slowed as he approached, obeying the traditional courtesy of the West. No stranger approached a homestead at the gallop, for haste was automatically associated with danger, and danger engendered fear. To honour the laws of the land, a rider approached slowly, so that he might be studied, appraised, then made welcome or treated with reserved hostility.

Gunn passed, slowly, under the portals which marked the outer boundary of the Santoz spread. A well-trodden track led towards the hacienda and outbuildings, a couple of miles further on. There was no sign of life, for this frontal approach to the hacienda was poor soil, incapable of sustaining crops or the roughest of fodder for horses or cattle. The rich, verdant pastures of the ranch lay behind the hacienda, extending outwards to both East and West for some twenty miles. There, the plentiful waters from the mountain streams of the San Orato hills fed the land all the year round, giving life and riches to its fortunate owner.

Twenty yards from the first of the ranch outbuildings, a low adobe wall ran the entire perimeter of the hacienda. As Gunn approached it, its seemingly bare top suddenly bristled with rifles and sombrero-topped heads.

'Come no farther, gringo,' barked out a warning voice.

Gunn reined his horse in immediately, lifting both hands well over his shoulders.

'What business have you here?' called the voice again. From behind the wall, a tall, lean Mexican stood up, the rifle in his hands pointed squarely at Gunn's chest.

'I have business with *Señor* Santoz. He should be expecting me. My name is Gunn,' Gunn retorted, calmly, a friendly smile on his face despite the inhospitable welcome.

The Mexican nodded thoughtfully, lowering the rifle. '*Si*, you are expected, *Señor* Gunn.'

As he spoke, his companions also stood up, each lowering their weapons. Gunn took this as an invitation to ride in. He spurred his mount into a slow trot and continued up to the hacienda.

Don Santoz came out on to the porch to welcome him. His face was smiling and apologetic. 'Please forgive the rude welcome, *Señor* Gunn,' he said warmly. 'Unfortunately, one can take no chances with strangers in these parts.' He held out his hand. 'I am Don Santoz. At your service.'

'I understand,' Gunn said pleasantly, accepting the offered handshake. 'John Cunningham has told of me?'

'*Si*,' Don Santoz nodded, as he gestured for Gunn to enter the hacienda. '*Señor* Cunningham wrote to me of your coming, and of your mission. It is unfortunate that you have had a wasted journey, *Señor* Gunn, but you are nevertheless a welcome and honoured guest. You shall stay with me as long as you wish.'

'A wasted journey?' Gunn queried as he followed Don Santoz into the opulently furnished study.

Santoz spread his hands expressively, shrugging his shoulders. 'Even were I willing to part with any of my precious stallions, I fear that you would not manage to take them more than two miles from here,' he said mysteriously, an apologetic look on his face. He crossed to a richly-carved rosewood bureau and picked up a crystal decanter. 'A glass of sherry, *Señor* Gunn? The finest of Spain – and surely not then good enough for a man who has come such a difficult and dangerous journey.'

Gunn nodded his head in acceptance. 'You are most generous, *Señor* Santoz.'

Don Santoz poured two healthy measures of sherry into two fine crystal goblets. Crossing the room, he handed one to Gunn, then raised his own glass in toast. 'Your health, *señor*.' He gestured to a plush leather settee, inviting Gunn to sit down.

Gunn made himself comfortable, sipping at his sherry politely for a few moments. After a while, he reached into his pocket and drew out a thin sheaf of papers, handing them across to Don Santoz. 'These are the bloodstock records of John Cunningham's mares,' he explained softly. 'Perhaps, *señor* Santoz, when you have studied them, you might be willing to reconsider your refusal to negotiate a breeding deal. I feel sure you will realise the fine breeding in the line, *señor*. Mixed with your own, almost legendary bloodstock, there lies the potential to produce perhaps the finest strain of horse ever seen on this continent. We would, of course, come to some mutual arrangement whereby you yourself acquired foals of this stock.'

Don Santoz, glanced through the bloodstock papers. Only his eyebrows betrayed the fact that he was suitably impressed. After a few seconds perusal, his face clouded again. He handed the papers back to Gunn with a sad shake of his head. 'Alas, it can not be, *señor* Gunn. As you say, the two bloods would mingle well. A most superior beast indeed could well be the outcome. But it is just not possible.'

His voice held genuine regret. Gunn was deeply puzzled. 'Perhaps you could explain, Don Santoz? I have no wish to appear rude, but I fail to understand.'

Don Santoz nodded sagely. 'Of course, *señor* Gunn.' He rose, crossing to the bureau and pouring another sherry. 'Did you have a safe and untroubled journey here, *señor* Gunn?' he asked suddenly returning.

Gunn shook his head, quickly explaining the brush with the noctural bandits.

Don Santoz smiled sadly, once again extending his hands in a gesture which seemed to express a complete answer. 'And there you have it, in a nutshell, as I believe you Americans say. The countryside for miles around is swarming with these bandidos. You are fortunate to have reached this hacienda alive. You would certainly not escape from it with a Santoz stallion. My black

35

horses are a rich prize indeed, *señor* Gunn. There are many who desire them. They would steal, even kill for one such animal. You saw for yourself that I have to guard my hacienda at all times with a private militia.'

Gunn was astounded. 'Your stallions are that valuable?'

Don Santoz smiled bitterly. 'Not, perhaps, in your American terms of money,' he explained. 'Here in Mexico, their value is measured in blood. Those black stallions are the centre of a bitter and longstanding blood feud, *señor* Gunn. It has been going on for generations. I inherited it, and I will pass it on to my own children.'

'What happened?' Gunn's curiosity was aroused. It got the better of his good manners.

Don Santoz did not seem to mind, however. Perhaps he felt that it was something of a relief to share the story with a stranger. A distant look on his bronzed face preceded the telling of it. 'My great-grandfather gathered together all this land,' he started. 'It was not easy, and many men had to die before some semblance of order came to these parts. But although he was a hard man, my forbearer was also fair. He shared his land with many small and poorer families, allotting them portions of land as tenant farmers, taking only a small proportion of the harvest as reward. One year, the crops were destroyed by fire. Many believe that the fire was deliberately started by one of the families – the Estuartis – in a vain attempt to boost the value of their own crop. If this was so, it failed, for the fire spread everywhere, and destroyed everything. There was great hunger and poverty that year. Many children died. My great-grandfather drove the Estuarti family from this land, impounding their few meagre possessions as a penance. They had only one thing of any value – a fine black stallion. It was that horse which sired the breed which I maintain to this day. The descendants of Miguel Estuarti are sworn by blood and birthright to reclaim them, and wipe the name of Santoz forever from this land.'

36

Gunn was amazed. 'A blood feud? After three generations?'

Don Santoz smiled faintly again. 'I see you do not understand, *señor* Gunn,' he murmured quietly. 'You must realise that we are a proud people. Our pride is a fierce one, so much so that it may well be a sin. If so, then it is our curse, it remains with us, and can not be driven away.'

Gunn fell silent. Don Santoz stared at him broodingly for a few moments before speaking again. 'So you see, *señor* Gunn, that you could never hope to take a single horse of that breed away from this place. You would be tracked all the way back to the border. Today, the name of Estuarti is carried only by the last male heir – young Gomez. He leads a band of desperados, who plunder and kill for their survival in this harsh land. It is probable that the three bandidos who attacked you were some of his men. If so, you are already a marked man, *señor*. You arrived here alive, but you may never reach the border when you return.' He rose, the story finished. 'Come, *señor*. Now you must meet my family, as my honoured guest. My wife, and my two fine daughters.'

'You have no son?' Gunn asked.

Don Santoz shook his head sadly. 'Alas *señor* Gunn – my family also dies with this generation. When I die, or Gomez Estuarti is killed, the blood feud is over forever. That, perhaps, is why Gomez fights so desperately to avenge his family before it is too late. Why I must defend myself so forcefully.'

He gestured towards the door. Gunn rose, following his host out of the study and towards the main living room of the spacious hacienda. His mind was deeply troubled at Don Santoz' last words. It seemed he had a slim chance indeed of returning safely, if a whole band of Mexican bandits lay out there in the desert plotting his destruction.

Chapter Five

It was not only in the Mexican desert that men planned James Gunn's downfall. Back in Sagebrush Flats, the Shobrook family were also engaged in a council of war. Jess, Wesley and Brendan Shobrook sat around the kitchen table, their faces black with rage.

'I say we just ride on out to the Cunningham place and shoot the sonavabitch down,' Brendan growled, slamming his clenched fist down upon the table. Of the three brothers, he was the oldest, but also the most hot-headed.

Jess, the youngest, shook his head slowly. 'No, that ain't the way,' he muttered. 'It might not work out quite the way we wanted it.'

Brendan turned on his younger brother with scorn. 'You reckon to just let him get away with gunning down poor Conrad like that?'

Wesley intervened. 'Let the boy say his piece, Bren.' He turned to Jess. 'You got a plan, boy?'

Jess nodded thoughtfully. 'Yep,' he retorted. 'I got a plan.'

'Out with it then, Jess,' Brendan snapped testily, as the youngster fell silent, a cunning smile on his face.

'Well, the way I see it, going after him with shooting irons ain't a wise plan,' Jess observed. 'You two forget, but I'm the only one who's seen Gunn in action. I saw him shoot – and he's pure dynamite. Even the three of us couldn't guarantee getting him clean, without maybe getting shot up ourselves. That being so, I figger to let someone else do the job for us.'

'You mean bring in a gunslinger?' Wesley asked. His voice was tinged with disgust, implying his young brother's cowardice.

Jess shook his head violently. 'No, Wes, I figger we can get the sheriff to string him up,' he said chillingly. 'Way I see it, hanging ain't none too bad for him, after what he done to poor Conrad.'

Brendan Shobrook let out a derisive snort. 'Call that an idea, Jess,' he scoffed. 'I heard better plans from a new-born babe. Why, you heard sheriff Baines yourself, Jess. Ain't nothing he can do against Gunn. Sam Lake started the trouble, it was pure self defence.'

An evil grin had settled over Jess Shobrook's face. 'Won't be nothing to do with the shooting,' he said mysteriously. 'We get Gunn strung up for something else altogether.' He broke off, looking into each brother's eyes in turn, proud of himself. 'Horse-thievin's a hanging offence, right?'

Brendan and Wesley nodded slowly in agreement.

'Right. So we make Mister Gunn a sneaky horse-thief.' Jess finished, triumphantly. 'That way, we get to see him hung in public – all nice and legal, like.'

'But Gunn ain't no horse-thief,' Wesley put in, not understanding the animal cunning of his younger sibling.

Jess threw him a scathing glance. 'You ain't none too fast on the uptake, Wes,' he said, cuttingly. 'We make it our business to convince folks different.'

There was silence for a while as Jess left his brothers to assimilate the idea.

'OK. Jess. What's your plan?' Brendan asked, after a while.

Jess laughed openly, knowing that he had won the day. 'Now here's what we do,' he muttered. 'Tonight, late, we ride out to the Sorenson ranch. Right now, Brendan gets busy doing a little metal work.'

The Sorenson ranch-house was dark and silent as the three horsemen trotted slowly and quietly towards it.

In the corrals, the horses snickered and whinnied fretfully at the approach of the nocturnal visitors.

Jess Shobrook led his mount to the corral fence and slipped out of the saddle. He crept stealthily to the gate, unhitching it and pushing it open. Walking in, he roped up three of the Sorenson horses and led them gently outside, hitching them behind his own mount. He looked up at Brendan, his mouth pursed in a whisper. 'You and Wes ride out now. I got one more little chore to attend to.'

The two brothers obeyed, wheeling their horses silently and trotting away as silently as they had come. When the last faint footfall had faded completely, Jess Shobrook reached to his gun-belt and drew his Smith and Wesson. Gun in hand, he crept across the ground towards the bunk-house.

Reaching it, he gently pushed open the door and crept inside. The faint sound of snoring came to his ears. Guided by the sound, he made his way in the darkness until he stood over the bedroll of old Elmer Garson, the Sorenson family's only hired hand.

Jess cocked the hammer of his gun with a faint click. The noise was enough to wake the old-timer, who sat up suddenly, his eyes wide with fear. He recognised the shadowy figure hovering over him at once. 'Why, Jess boy, what in tarnation d'ya think you're doing?'

They were the last words the old-timer ever uttered. Jess's finger tightened on the trigger. 'Sorry, Elmer. Ain't nothing personal,' he muttered under his breath. The words were drowned by the crashing roar of the Smith and Wesson as he calmly planted a slug deep in the old man's brain.

The murderous job completed, Jess ran outside to his horse and threw himself into the saddle. At full gallop, he rode away from the Sorenson ranch, dragging the three stolen horses behind him. As he rode, he grinned wickedly to himself. The first part of his evil plan had gone off without a hitch – but the night's work was not yet over. There was one more task to complete before he could sit back to wait for Gunn's date with the noose.

He caught up with his two brothers, slowing his horse and indicating for them to follow him. He swerved off the main trail, cutting out across the surrounding wasteland in the general direction of the Cunningham spread.

'Heard a shot, Jess,' Wesley asked, his voice troubled. 'What happened?'

'Old Elmer musta heard us,' Jess lied. 'He came out after me with a shotgun. I had to shoot the poor devil.'

Wesley sighed heavily. 'Didn't plan on no shootings, Jess,' he complained sadly.

Jess laughed softly under his breath. 'Neither did I,' he lied again. 'But it sure works out well.'

'How do you figger that, Jess?'

'A man might just talk hisself out of a horse-thieving rap,' Jess observed. 'But he'll hang for a murder, sure as hell.'

Wesley fell silent. For a minute, a horrible suspicion flowered in his mind, but he pushed it aside. He could not believe anything quite so evil about his young brother. The shooting was just an unfortunate accident, that was all. It was a terrible pity though – for old Elmer was a likeable old cuss who had never harmed a fly. The people of Sagebrush Flats would be very bitter about his killing.

In silence, the three brothers headed towards the Cunningham ranch. Jess Shobrook was feeling mighty pleased with himself. Things were working out just as he had planned. There was a stiff breeze blowing up, which would have removed all traces of their trail from the ground by morning. By that time, the last two stages of the plot would be completed, and James Gunn's fate would be sealed. The Shobrook family would take a terrible revenge for the death of their brother.

41

Chapter Six

Gunn's stay at the Santoz hacienda was not destined to be a peaceful one. The morning after his arrival started with trouble.

The family were seated around the huge mahogany table, eating a sumptuous breakfast. Gunn sat at the head of the table – a gesture made by Don Santoz in deference to his position of honoured guest. Beside him, Don Santoz' eldest daughter Rosita sat, frequently breaking off from her meal to cast him wickedly flirtatious glances.

She was a real Spanish beauty – with glossy, jet-black hair which hung down to her waist in thick waves and dark, flashing eyes which could start a man's stomach churning. Her rich, glowing colouring only served to emphasise her beauty, adding to it a quality of almost animal-like sex-appeal which belied her strict Catholic upbringing. She appeared almost wanton at times, when her dark eyes glowed with unashamed admiration for Gunn's rugged physique and his striking good looks. Whenever Gunn's eyes fell upon her, Rosita's lush red lips seemed to be curled into a seductive smile which held the promise of passionate kisses.

Gunn found her obvious attentions to him highly embarrassing. Many times, he nervously glanced away when her eyes fell upon him, desperately attempting to strike up some banal conversation with Don Santoz, his wife, or the young 14-year-old daughter. Whenever he did so, he was acutely aware of Rosita's dark eyes approving him, or of her father's faint but unmistakable glances of concern.

From outside the hacienda, the crackle of gunfire suddenly disturbed the family meal. Don Santoz leapt to his feet, dabbing at his mouth with a napkin before pushing his chair away hurriedly and reaching for the gun he wore on his hip.

'Bandidos,' he hissed urgently, his face creased with worry. He rushed towards the door, with Gunn hot on his heels.

The hacienda was under attack. Outside the protective adobe wall, some twenty mounted bandits were circling, rifles blazing. Don Santoz' men returned the fire as best they could, but the constant hail of lead made it dangerous, if not downright suicidal, to rise from their protection to take sight on a clear target. As Gunn took in the scene, two of the guards fell back screaming, as heavy slugs chewed into their bodies.

Don Santoz dropped to a crouch, running across the open courtyard and throwing himself down behind the wall where the last man had fallen. Gunn glanced across to the corral, where his horse was tethered. His Springfield rifle was still tucked into its saddle holster.

A stray bullet sang past his ear, chipping a hunk of plaster from the wall of the hacienda behind him. Gunn dived to the ground instinctively, flattening himself on his belly. More rifle bullets ploughed into the dusty soil, spewing up dirt and loose pebbles as he slithered like a snake across the courtyard towards the corral.

Reaching it, Gunn looked up. He appeared to be out of the main line of fire. The bandits were concentrating on the defenders behind the wall, picking them off with their heads. Feeling reasonably safe, Gunn stood up and made a dash into the corral. Once inside, the bodies of the horses afforded him plenty of protection. He made his way quickly to his own mount, slipping the Springfield out of its holster and delving into his saddle-bag for a good handful of spare cartridges. Tucking them safely into his pocket, he turned away and searched for a suitable vantage point. His keen eyes found the ideal place. On top of the flat-roofed hacienda, there was a small balcony, its perimeter guarded by a low, turretted wall. From there, Gunn figured, he could pick off the Mexican horsemen at will, counting on their inferior marksmanship to keep him comparatively safe himself.

The only immediate problem was in climbing to the balcony without getting shot. There was no protection on the way up, and the entire area of that wall was already heavily chipped and scarred with the impact of bullets.

Gunn made up his mind to risk it. Running to the corral gate, he closed it again quickly, to prevent the panicking horses bolting out to add to the confusion. At a crouch, he ran full pelt back across the open court-yard, weaving and zig-zagging from side to side. His movements did not go unnoticed. Less than half-way to the hacienda, a couple of the bandits picked him out as a prime target, and a dozen little spumes of dust around his flying feet marked the unnerving nearness of their shots.

He reached the wall safely and began to climb up the jutting end-stones at the corner. Slugs cracked into the white plaster beside and above him, sending splinters flying in all directions. Dust got into Gunn's eyes, nearly blinding him with its burning alkaline content. Still he kept climbing, his arms and legs going like pistons. He reached the parameter of the balcony and threw himself over it to safety as a half dozen more slugs found their mark within inches of his head.

Protected now, Gunn paused only to spit onto his fingers and wipe out his eyes before settling down on his belly and resting the barrel of the Springfield over the castellated ledge. He peered down the sights, pick-ing out his first victim and taking careful aim. He squeezed the trigger gently. His target jerked in the saddle as Gunn's bullet slammed into his chest. Fling-ing his arms in the air, the Mexican toppled backwards from his horse to sprawl in the dust.

Gunn allowed himself a faint smile of satisfaction.

From his high position, the Mexicans were sitting ducks. He squinted down the sights again, seeking his next victim.

As he squeezed the trigger, the bandit he was aiming at bought a horrible death. There was a bright flash of flame from his chest, accompanied by a sharp report Gunn's bullet had hit the bandolier of ammunition which crossed his chest, the impact detonating several of the cartridges in it. With a hole the size of a man's fist blown out of his ribcage, the Mexican fell to join his companion, his blood turning the dust into a red mud.

Two more shots followed, claiming as many new victims. Gunn aimed the rifle slowly and deliberately, concentrating on sniping off specific targets rather than fire at random, as most of the defenders were doing. It was a policy which soon paid off. As Gunn stopped firing to reload his rifle for the third time, the circling bandits were already beginning to back off, leaving behind a dozen dead and dying.

The brisk crackle of gunfire died down, finally ceasing altogether. Gunn watched the bandits ride away, well clear of rifle range. Only when he was satisfied that they would not be coming back in the near future did he climb down from his vantage point and join Don Santoz by the adobe wall.

Don Santoz checked the wounded quickly, calling into the house for help. His wife and Rosita came out almost immediately, bearing clean bandages and bowls of hot water. They set about tending the injured men. As Gunn walked to his side, Don Santoz was directing six more of his men to deal with the bodies of the bandits scattered out in the desert. Two of the men walked between the bodies, prodding each one with their boots dispassionately. The dead ones they left alone. Those only wounded were quickly despatched with a bullet through the temple. The job finished, the two executioners joined their comrades in digging a pit for a mass grave.

Don Santoz caught the slightly shocked look on Gunn's face as he watched the callous killings, and smiled thinly. 'They are bandidos, *señor* Gunn,' he murmured by way of explanation. 'If they recovered from their wounds, they would be hanged. Even worse, they could be imprisoned for twenty years. You have seen the inside of a Mexican prison, *señor?*'

Gunn shook his head. Don Santoz pulled a disapproving face. 'It is better they be dead, *señor* Gunn. Believe me.'

Gunn dropped the subject. 'Are these attacks frequent?' he asked.

Don Santoz shook his head sadly. 'They have never attacked like this in broad daylight,' he said quietly. 'Some raids at night, the isolated ambush when my men go for supplies, perhaps one or two bandidos riding within rifle range and sniping at my guards. Nothing more than that, up to now. This full-scale attack may well be the start of things to come, I fear.'

'Will they be back?'

Don Santoz shrugged. 'Who knows? Gomez may have shown us his full strength, or he may merely have brought a small party to confuse us. There may be twenty bandidos in the hills, or there may be two hundred. They may return, they may not. With bandidos, *señor*, one never knows anything for sure, except that they will kill and steal whenever the opportunity arises.' He broke off to clap Gunn on the shoulder. 'But I am discourteous, *señor* Gunn. I owe you my thanks for your help. You shot well. Without your sure aim, things might have gone differently for us.'

Gunn glanced around at the dead and wounded. Don Santoz had lost four of his guards, and a further seven were wounded. Two of those were unlikely to pull through. The rest could be fighting again in three or four days. Don Santoz was right. It could have been a lot worse.

That was looking at the positive side of things. On the other hand, if Don Santoz' gloomiest alternative were true, the bandits might be strong enough to descend in a horde, standing every chance of slaughtering everyone within the walls of the Santoz hacienda. It was not a reassuring thought. Gunn turned to his host. 'I think you need some additional fortifications.'

Don Santoz shrugged hopelessly. 'I agree, but what can I do?'

Gunn racked his brains, staring pensively out across the wasteland in front of him. A sudden idea struck home. 'Have you any dynamite here?' he asked. 'Blasting powder, anything like that?'

Don Santoz thought for a moment, then nodded affirmatively. 'There is a little. A box or two which I bought to blast out a new water reservoir to catch the Spring rains. It is a job I have not managed to get around to just yet.'

'Good.' For once, Gunn was thankful that the Mexican tradition of 'manyana' had been followed. It gave them a chance. 'Perhaps you would be good enough to bring the explosives to me, Don Santoz,' he said. 'We can lay a little surprise for Gomez and his cutthroats.'

'Of course.' Don Santoz barked orders to the two nearest men, then looked up at Gunn with a puzzled expression. 'What have you in mind, *señor* Gunn?'

Gunn smiled secretively. 'You'll see,' he answered.

Don Santoz smiled apologetically. 'I am sorry that you have become involved in my family feud,' he said quietly. 'And it is good of you to offer your help. I am indebted to you.'

Gunn made no reply as the two hands reappeared with two boxes of blasting charges. The burial party were just returning, having dumped the twelve bodies of the dead bandits into a communal pit and covered it over. Gunn took a couple of shovels from their hands as they walked past. 'Come on, we have some work to do,' he murmured to Don Santoz, gesturing out into the desert. He led the way, the two hands carrying the explosives behind him.

Gunn walked a good way from the protective walls

surrounding the hacienda before he started to dig. He made a shallow trench, carefully buried a small charge, then just covered it again with soil. He marked the position of the buried explosive with a small ring of pebbles. Don Santoz soon got the idea. He dug the holes, whilst Gunn placed the charges and prepared them in the same manner. When the two men had finished, the whole area was a huge minefield, booby-trapped with over thirty caches of explosive.

Satisfied with his handiwork, Gunn straightened up, stretching his aching bones. 'That ought to ensure we give them a warm welcome if they call again,' he muttered. He followed Don Santoz back to the hacienda to finish off his rudely interrupted breakfast.

Rosita caught him by the arm as he walked into the hacienda. Her dark eyes were sparkling with admiration. 'You are a brave man, James Gunn,' she whispered. 'Brave as well as handsome.'

Gunn shook the compliment aside with an embarrassed smile. Rosita squeezed his arm, brushing her body against his. Still holding tightly, she led him into the dining room.

Gunn caught the disapproving look on Don Santoz' face and got the message. Mexican hospitality did not extend to encouraging liaisons between daughters and visiting *gringos* . . . even if the master of the house was indebted to them.

Don Santoz finished his breakfast and pushed away his plate. He wiped his mouth and stood up. 'Come, *señor* Gunn, it is time I showed you what you came these many miles to see.' He led the way out of the back of the hacienda. 'There,' he said proudly, stepping outside and pointing to a solidly-built stone corral.

Gunn followed his pointing finger, and a feeling of awe rose in his throat as he saw the string of famous black stallions for the first time. There were over a score of them, and even from a distance. Gunn could see that they were the most magnificent beasts he had

48

ever laid eyes on. Eagerly, he followed Don Santoz over to the corral to admire the captive horses at closer range.

They were magnificent animals indeed. Looking at their sleek, jet-black manes and the moulded symmetry of their strong, perfectly-formed bodies, Gunn could begin to understand his host's fierce pride in them, and John Cunningham's obsession with breeding them. It even made the feud of blood seem more understandable, if not excusable.

Don Santoz looked up at Gunn, begging a compliment. Gunn was not slow to give him what he desired. 'They were well-worth the journey – if only to see them,' he muttered. The words were not entirely an exaggeration.

Don Santoz looked at the stallions lovingly for a few more seconds, then turned away abruptly. 'Now you have seen the Santoz stallions, my friend,' he said quietly. 'Alas, that is all I can do for you – merely to show them off.'

'I understand, Don Santoz,' Gunn murmured. It was a lie, but it seemed to pacify the nobleman for the time being.

'Now I must check my men and their weapons,' Don Santoz said, striding back towards the hacienda. 'If Gomez and his men do not return today, they will surely attempt another raid after dark.'

'I'll help you.' Gunn had already decided that he was going to give the guards a few lessons in target practice. His own life was at stake, along with all the members of the Santoz household, and the shooting he had seen left a lot to be desired.

Don Santoz accepted his offer gratefully, leaving Gunn with a bunch of the guards whilst he returned inside the hacienda to count the remaining ammunition and guns.

Gunn spent a busy, if somewhat unproductive afternoon. Making the guards understand was difficult, since few of them spoke clear English, and their concept of gun warfare seemed to be to make as much noise as possible and pray to the many saints that their random bullets found targets. They did not take well to the idea of holding their fire, picking out only specific targets and thus conserving valuable ammunition. In the end, Gunn gave it up as a bad job. As ever, he could only rely on his own weaponry to protect his own skin.

The afternoon passed lazily away. An hour or so before sundown, one of the guards at the wall let out a warning shout. Gunn was inside the hacienda, taking full advantage of its cool, shady interior. He rushed outside into the courtyard.

The guard was pointing excitedly out over the desert. Gunn shielded his eyes against the glare of the dying sun and strained his eyes. All he could see was a massive swirling dust cloud, some five or six miles away.

Don Santoz ran up beside him, also peering out across the wasteland.

'What is it?' Gunn queried. The sun was bright, and its low, sloping rays were directed straight into his eyes.

'It is either a dust storm, or a very large group of horsemen. Whichever it is, it is headed this way,' Don Santoz replied, heavily.

His tone told him not to count too much on the first possibility. The bandits were making a second attack. This time, they had come in full force, and had chosen their time shrewdly. Coming out of the setting sun, they could take full advantage of the fact. All those within the hacienda walls would be almost blinded, whilst the bandits would be free to pick out their targets with no difficulty at all.

Gunn decided to take no chances. As Don Santoz ordered his men to take up their defensive positions, Gunn raced into the hacienda, grabbed his rifle and made the climb up to the balcony for the second time that day. Settling himself down, he waited to see what the approaching dust-cloud would disgorge.

The faint thunder of distant hoofbeats came to his ears before he could see clearly through the swirling dust. Then the riders became visible, and a cold chill struck Gunn right to the heart. There were well over a hundred bandits riding upon the hacienda. This time, Gomez Estuarti obviously intended to finish the job for all time. If the bandits were allowed to penetrate the outer defensive wall, it would be a bloody massacre. As the riders came nearer, Gunn settled himself more comfortably upon his stomach, cursing the brightness of the sun. He lined up the sights of the Springfield upon the furthest circle of stones, his eyes half-closed to shut out as much light as possible as he squinted along the barrel.

All the charges had been placed well outside accurate range of hand-guns, but not of Gunn's rifle. He waited until the first wave of horsemen passed the buried charge before squeezing off two shots into the very centre of the circle.

The second shot did it. With a mighty explosion, the charge detonated, sending the surrounding pebbles flying in all directions – as deadly as any shrapnel from a Hotchkiss gun. The initial blast tore the soft underbellies of two horses to shreds, in a misty cloud of blood. Their riders plunged headfirst over the saddlehorns, and down the sides of the stricken beasts necks. Either side of them, the flying debris found other fleshy targets. Two Mexicans screamed shrilly as jagged pieces of stone ripped into their bodies, gouging out terrible sacrifices of flesh. Several other riders were thrown from their saddles as their mounts reared in panic, taken utterly by surprise by the deafening explosion.

Gunn reviewed the success of his first charge with mixed emotions. He felt sick to his stomach at the idea of killing and maiming innocent horses, but it was a matter of sheer survival. Swallowing his finer feelings, he took careful aim on a second buried cache of explosive.

It caused even more confusion amongst the charging Mexicans. As the explosion shook the ground, dozens of riders reined in their mounts, desperate to maintain control before the beasts bolted, and unsure of where to head next. It seemed that no inch of the desert was safe to them. In their panic and confusion, virtually all movement stopped for a few minutes. It made them sitting targets.

Gunn's Springfield barked again and again, setting off the buried explosives with uncanny regularity. The Mexican bandits were trapped and helpless, blinded by the flying dust and at the mercy of their terrified horses. Those who were not killed or maimed by the explosions, or cut down by the withering hail of fire which came from within the hacienda walls were thrown from their mounts, many meeting death as they plunged headfirst into the unforgiving surface of the desert floor.

At last, the dust was so thick that Gunn could see no more of his makeshift targets. He had detonated perhaps two dozen of the charges; a further six remained untouched.

In the comparative silence which fell as the booming roar of the explosions ceased, the crackle of gunfire seemed little more than the chirping of crickets. The swirling dust gradually settled, and as the bandits saw the carnage around them, a secondary panic broke loose amongst their ranks. They were no longer an organised band – just a frightened, desperate rabble. Individual riders took control of their mounts and scattered in all directions. Many of the bandits fled on foot, having either been thrown from their saddles or felt their mounts blasted to death beneath them.

Gunn reloaded the rifle and picked off three running figures in a row. Others dropped, screaming, as a fusillade of lead followed their flight from the battlefield.

The retreat was complete now. The muffled pounding of hooves on sand faded away into the distance. Slowly, the dust sank back to the ground and the full bloodbath was revealed. It was a scene of indescribable carnage. Dismembered and mutilated bodies lay thickly, wherever the eye fell. Wounded men and horses writhed in agony, terrible cries of agony filled the air. At a rough estimate, Gunn counted nearly fifty human bodies, and a score of dead and dying horses.

As he looked, his heart heavy, the men behind the hacienda walls stood, gazed out at their terrible victory and gave vent to a ragged cheer. Gunn turned his head away in revulsion. He felt no cause to celebrate such incredible slaughter.

Climbing down from the balcony, he walked into the hacienda as Don Santoz despatched his squad of executioners once again to finish off the wounded. He wanted no part of it, not even to see the final justice of total war. It was a purely Mexican thing, no quarter granted, nor asked for. It was not Gunn's way.

Rosita ran up to him, her rich colouring paled by what she had seen. There was no flirtatious smile in her eyes now. She grasped his arm, her voice slightly shaken. '*Señor* James, is there anything I can get for you.'

Gunn nodded curtly. 'A good, stiff drink, Rosita.'

The girl nodded understandingly, running off to fetch a good four finger measure of Tequila. Gunn took the glass from her hand gratefully, pouring the fiery spirit down his throat in one, swift movement. It served to burn his throat and stomach, but could not cauterise the heavy depression he felt in his heart.

Chapter Seven

John Cunningham looked up from his chores as the group of riders approached his ranch. He smiled, recognising Sheriff Baines, flanked by two deputies. Behind him rode Lars Sorenson, a friend despite the fact that he bred horses in the same area and was Cunningham's only real competitor.

He called into the house. 'Lydia, we got company. Put some coffee on the stove, will you?' Wiping his hands on his trousers, he walked out to greet his guests.

Sheriff Baines' face was grim.

'Tom, good to see you,' Cunningham said warmly, stretching up his hand to the man.

Baines made no attempt to accept the handshake. Silently, he slipped down from the saddle and regarded Cunningham coldly. 'This ain't a social call, John,' he muttered rather awkwardly. Baines felt annoyed with himself at having to treat John Cunningham in such an off-handed manner. They had been good friends for years, and his young son Michael rode a pony which had been a Thanksgiving present from the Cunningham stables. But all that had to be pushed to one side for the moment. Baines had a job to do; and at times it could be an unpleasant and thankless one. Right now, he had a murder on his hands and an anonymous note which incriminated the Cunningham ranch.

Cunningham's face clouded over, sensing the sheriff's grim mood. He could not understand. 'What's up, Tom?'

'Where's Gunn?' Baines shot straight back.

'Sent him to Mexico on business.' Cunningham replied

54

openly. 'Look, what's all this about, Tom. I guess I got a right to know.'

Still Baines could tell him nothing. 'Like to look around some, John,' he murmured quietly.

Cunningham spread his hands in an open invitation. 'You're welcome, Tom, you know that. I ain't got nothing to hide.'

Baines nodded. Looking up at Lars Sorenson, he beckoned him to dismount. 'Sorenson – you like to come with me please?'

The man dismounted, carefully avoiding Cunningham's eyes. The two men walked over to the corral, unfastened the gate and walked in. They walked amongst the horses, examining them carefully. After a while, Sorenson picked out three of them and gathered them together. Silently, he followed Baines out of the corral, leading the animals behind him.

Cunningham stared in disbelief at the three horses as the two men approached him. It was difficult to keep a sure check, when he had over a hundred horses in his care, but he was sure that he had never seen the piebald mare and the sorrel in the group before.

'What do you know about these, John,' sheriff Baines said in a chill voice.

Cunningham looked completely baffled. 'They certainly ain't mine,' he admitted. 'But I ain't got the faintest idea how they got into my corral.'

Baines bent down beside the horses, looking up sadly. 'They got your brand on 'em, Cunningham,' he muttered. 'Or at least, something which looks pretty much like a ringer for your brand.'

The sheriff's tone, and the way he had dropped the friendly use of Cunningham's first name told him that something was seriously wrong. An inner sense told him he was in bad trouble, but he could not even try to understand why. He bent beside Baines to look at the fresh brand marks on the three horses.

They looked odd, somehow – slightly blurred, and with some parts of the brand seemingly older than the

55

rest. Yet it was unmistakably the hallmark of the Circle 8 ranch – a figure eight surrounded by a plain ring.

'Hell, Baines, I got no idea where these horses came from,' Cunningham protested.

Sorenson broke his silence for the first time. 'They come from my corrals, John,' he murmured flatly. He knelt beside the first horse, his finger tracing over the scar tissue of the brand. 'There's my mark – the old part of that brand.' His index finger traced a figure 'S' in the Circle 8 brand. It was old scar tissue, healed over by time. The surrounding circle, and the other side of the 8 were still moist to the touch, bearing traces of fresh blood still seeping from the damaged flesh.

As Cunningham stared down in horror and disbelief, there was a shout from the bunkhouse. Baines' two deputies had been searching over there, and one of them was just returning with a long metal rod held high in his hand.

'Found it, Sheriff,' he cried. He ran over, handing the rod to Baines, who studied it carefully for a few seconds.

He showed Cunningham the business end of the metal rod. It was a running iron, all right, Cunningham saw that at a glance. A rogue branding iron, skilfully fashioned to change one mark into another. The incriminating piece of iron now stared him in the face – a circular outer ring, with a curved piece inside it. A curved iron specifically designed to change an 'S' into an '8'.

'Found it in Gunn's bunk, just as you was told,' the deputy told Baines. 'Guess that just about clinches it, don't it Sheriff?'

Sheriff Baines nodded his head sorrowfully. 'Yes, Luke, I guess it does.' He turned back to Cunningham. 'When did Gunn leave for Mexico?'

'Two days ago.'

Baines' sad expression deepened. 'You sure, Cunningham?'

'Of course I'm sure,' Cunningham shot back testily. 'Now what the hell is going on here?'

Baines nodded up towards the house. 'Will Lydia confirm that?'

'What?' demanded Cunningham angrily, his patience now completely shot to pieces. He didn't understand what was going on, and it worried him.

'That Gunn left for Mexico two days ago,' Baines said. 'If that's so, it puts you in a whole lot of trouble, Cunningham.'

'Yeah, Lydia will confirm it,' Cunningham said wearily. 'Now what the hell trouble are you talking about, Tom? I tell you I ain't got the faintest notion how them horses got that fake brand, or how the hell they got into my corral, but you sure as hell know I ain't no horse-thief, Tom. Dammit, man, you've known me long enough.'

Baines was confused himself. It was true. He had known John Cunningham for many years, and he had always had faith in him as an honest man. But now he was faced with overwhelming evidence to the contrary, and he had a dead, innocent old man in his morgue. The two situations just didn't mix.

'A man can always change,' he muttered, almost under his breath.

Cunningham was really worried now. He glanced up at Lars Sorenson, his voice pleading. 'Lars, you know, surely, that I wouldn't dream of stealing horses – let alone yours. Tell him, for God's sake. Tom Baines seems to have gone off his head.'

Sorenson looked down at him in pity. 'I know what I see, John,' he said miserably. 'I can't argue with my own eyes.'

Baines slipped his gun out of his holster. 'Gonna have to take you in, Cunningham.' His free hand pulled a pair of handcuffs from his belt.

'Goddammit Tom – you really have gone plumb loco,' Cunningham exploded. 'It's bad enough you can't believe me that this is all some crazy mistake. To top it all by pulling a gun on me and reckoning you gotta take me into town in irons is really going over the top. Hell, even if I was guilty of horse-thieving, you'd leave a man to tend his property until the trial came up.'

Sheriff Baines' voice was heavy. 'I ain't charging you with rustling Cunningham. I'm charging you with murder.'

For the first time, Cunningham fully realised just how deep in trouble he really was, and that the events of the past ten minutes were not just some crazy day-dream. His whole body sagged wearily. In a daze, he held out his hands while Baines snapped the cuffs on his wrists.

Lydia came out onto the porch, smiling. 'Coffee's up,' she called, before her eyes took in what was happening. She rushed up, her face full of fear.

'Tom, is this some kind of joke?'

Sheriff Baines averted his eyes from her gaze. 'Sorry, Lydia,' he murmured under his breath. He turned away, pushing Cunningham towards the corral. 'Get your horse, Cunningham.'

Lydia broke down, screaming, as the men rode off towards town. What had just happened was impossible, yet it had happened just the same. She was utterly broken. She watched the riders fade into the distance through misted, tear-filled eyes, before staggering back into the ranch-house and throwing herself across the bed to sob herself to sleep.

Chapter Eight

From outside, the Santoz hacienda looked quietly asleep for the night, but this was far from the case. Although Don Santoz hardly expected a night attack after the bloody rout of the day, he was taking no chances. There was a watchful guard at virtually every window, and a dozen men patrolled the perimeter walls. If Gomez Estuarti could rally his gang of bandits – in itself unlikely – he would meet a determined and concerted opposition all through the hours of darkness.

Gunn finished his own two hour guard duty and headed for his room to get some much-needed sleep. It had been an exhausting day, both physically and mentally. He took off his boots, but kept his outer clothing on and a primed rifle by the bedside. Laying down, he stretched his long body out upon the bed and waited for sleep to come. He was sure it would not be long.

He had only just dropped off when the faintest creaking of his bedroom door snapped him into wakefulness again. Gunn's eyes peered through the gloom as the door began to inch open. A shadowy figure crept stealthily into the room towards Gunn's bed.

He moved like a spring uncoiling – in one smooth bound, Gunn leapt from the bed and grasped out at his nocturnal visitor, his fingers seeking the area where the throat should be. They encountered some loose, flimsy material which ripped at once.

His mysterious visitor gave a little scream. A female scream. Gunn recognised Rosita Santoz' voice as she spoke in a frightened whisper.

Señor James, it is only I . . . Rosita.'

Gunn dropped his hand, reaching to the bedside table and striking a lucifer. He applied it to the oil lamp, turning up the flame until a dim glow lit the room.

Rosita crossed her arms across her body, trying to cover up the large area of her exposed chest where the thin material of her nightgown had been ripped away. She did not fully accomplish the task. Her smooth, soft shoulders and the top swelling of her firm young breasts were clearly visible. Gunn tried to be a gentleman, averting his eyes. It wasn't easy.

'What are you doing here?' he hissed, not quite angrily.

Rosita lowered her eyes in shame. 'I am sorry. I could not sleep. I wanted to talk to you.'

Gunn grinned ruefully. 'The middle of the night is hardly the time to talk, Rosita,' he pointed out.

Too late, he heard the tread of heavy boots approaching his room. Gunn's heart dropped to his stomach as an angry voice boomed out.

'So. This is how my hospitality is repaid.'

Don Santoz stood framed in the door. His face was black with rage. Rosita, startled by her father's sudden appearance, whirled around to face him. As she moved, her arms dropped. She faced her father with her breasts fully exposed.

'Go to your room at once.' Don Santoz' voice was heavy, and trembling with rage.

Rosita obeyed the curt command with a little sob of fear, throwing Gunn an apologetic look before running from the room. Don Santoz looked squarely at Gunn, the corners of his mouth twitching nervously. '*Señor* Gunn. I took you to be a gentleman. I was wrong. You bring shame on my house, sir.'

Gunn hastened to explain, convince Don Santoz that it was all a ghastly mistake, but it was no use. The man was blinded by his aggrieved pride. He would listen to no words of explanation. He cut Gunn short as he started to speak. 'I will hear nothing from you, *Señor*

Gunn. You have brought dishonour on this house and my family. I swear by God that I shall avenge that honour by your death. At dawn, *Señor* Gunn, you shall meet me in duel.'

He reached out and slapped Gunn across the face. Gunn reeled back under the stinging blow, but made no attempt to retaliate. A thin trickle of blood dribbled from the side of his mouth.

Without another word, Don Santoz turned briskly on his heel and strode off, slamming Gunn's door behind him. Stunned, Gunn could only sink to his bed hopelessly, his mind reeling as the man's footsteps faded away down the corridor.

He lay awake for several hours, trying to put the ghastly business into some sort of order. Finally, slightly comforted by the hope that Don Santoz might be calmer and more willing to listen to reason in the morning, Gunn let his weariness creep over him again. He fell into a deep sleep.

Rough hands shook him awake. Gunn blinked the sleep from his eyes, staring up at the two men who stood over his bed in surprise. As full consciousness dawned, the events of the previous night came back to his mind. So it had not been a crazy dream, after all.

'Don Santoz awaits you in his study,' one of the men barked gruffly.

Gunn swung his long legs slowly over the side of the bed, bending down to pull on his boots. He stood, crossed to the water jug and basin on the far side of his room and splashed his face. Still the two men stood, mutely, beside his bed. Their taut, impassive faces betrayed nothing. Gunn finished his toilet, re-crossed to his bed and prepared to finish dressing. He reached out for his gunbelt, lying on the bedside table.

'You will not need that, *Señor* Gunn,' one of the guards snapped in an icy tone. To reinforce his words, his hand dropped to the butt of the Smith & Wesson which hung from his hip.

Gunn straightened, his face set in a grim mask. He

strode towards the door, the two Mexicans following closely behind him.

Don Santoz stood behind his desk awaiting him. His anger did not appear to have abated. His eyes were heavy and puffed, betraying the fact that he had not slept well.

The two guards ushered Gunn into the study, then discreetly backed out of the door, closing it silently. Gunn and Don Santoz faced each other quietly for several seconds. It was Gunn who broke the silence.

'Look, Don Santoz, last night was not what you thought. It was all an accident – a totally innocent mistake.'

'Enough!' Don Santoz' voice cracked like a whip. 'I will hear no lies or excuses for your outrageous conduct.' He produced a slim walnut box from his desk drawer, opening it. Nestling inside were a brace of matched duelling pistols. Don Santoz gestured to the guns, then to a pair of rapiers which adorned the wall. 'Your choice of weapons, *Señor* Gunn.'

Gunn's desperation boiled up inside him. The man's stupid, fierce pride was making him blind to reason. A duel was out of the question, ridiculous.

'There can be no question of us duelling, Don Santoz.' Gunn forced himself to speak in a calm voice. 'I have told you it was a mistake. You must believe me.'

Don Santoz clenched his teeth. 'You will fight with me, *Señor* Gunn,' he hissed coldly. 'You will give me the opportunity to avenge my family honour or I swear by God I shall have you shot like a dog.'

Gunn could see that it was hopeless. He tried another tack. '*Señor* Santoz, you told me yesterday that you considered yourself in my debt,' he reminded the man quietly. 'Now I call upon you to repay that debt . . . by putting all thoughts of this foolish duel out of your mind.'

It was the wrong thing to say. The man's eyes blazed with loathing and fury. 'By God, you are not only a rogue but a coward,' he spat out. 'You could lower yourself to redeem such a debt in order to save your miserable life.'

The words stung, but Gunn steeled himself to ignore them. Letting his own pride loose could only make matters worse. He tried again. 'You will not honour your debt?'

'I will not.' The words were flat, and final.

'Very well.' Gunn slumped in resignation. 'I am no coward, Don Santoz. I do not wish to duel with you because I have done no wrong in your house. However, you leave me no choice. I choose the rapiers.'

'So be it,' Don Santoz snapped, crossing to the wall and pulling down the weapons. 'One of my men will serve as your second, *Señor* Gunn. Now, if you are ready, we will ride out to a suitable place.' He gestured to the door.

Outside, the morning light was not yet complete. The air was crisp and cool, with low cloud hanging on the horizon. It looked like being a gloomy day. Perhaps it was a portent, Gunn mused as he saddled up.

His heart was heavy as they rode well away from the hacienda, towards the hills. The only slim ray of hope that remained in his mind lay in his choice of the rapiers as the duelling weapons. With luck, Gunn might be able to disarm Don Santoz, forcing him to yield. Failing that, he could only hope to let the man deal him a superficial wound, and count on the tradition of first blood to satisfy the proud Spaniard's honour. Neither seemed very likely. Don Santoz was not a man to be easily appeased.

The four riders headed towards a clump of boulders at the foot of the hills. They were arranged in a rough circle, creating a natural arena in the wilderness. Don Santoz drew up his horse, dismounting. The two guards flanked Gunn closely, as if prepared for him to attempt a cowardly flight.

Gunn slid down from his horse and faced his adversary. He made one more appeal to reason. 'I ask you once more to forget this pointless duel,' he murmured, not really expecting any results.

He was right. Don Santoz merely lay the two rapiers upon the ground and nodded at Gunn. 'Choose your weapon, *Señor.*'

Sighing wearily, Gunn bent and grasped the nearest sword, weighing and balancing it experimentally in his hand. It was a superb weapon, crafted in fine Toledo steel of great antiquity. It felt good in his hand, Gunn mused idly. At any other time, he would have felt enthused to have such a sword at his command, experienced the thrill of matching his skill and dexterity against another man. Fencing had been one of his great joys, the art of the thrust and parry one of his better talents. Alas, no safety-tipped foils and protective padding now. The rapiers were honed to perfection, their tips and sides razor-sharp to slice through flesh like hot knives through tallow. They were weapons of death, not of sport.

Don Santoz took up a fighting stance. Gunn glanced at the position of his feet, taking his measure of the man. It was obvious that Don Santoz was an aggressive swordsman, taking the initiative and making all the play, Gunn's trained eye told him. That much was good, for Gunn had always had a slight edge over most men when it came to defensive manouevres. He was quick on his feet, with a lithe, graceful action which could take his whole body dancing mere fractions of an inch clear of slicing steel. As a man committed to attacking swordsmanship, Don Santoz was put at an immediate disadvantage. He could be tired more easily, led on to the point where the light rapier in his hand would become a heavy burden, and his finer senses dulled to the point of confusion. He was also a much older man than Gunn, and experience was not always a fair substitute for stamina in duelling.

With all this in mind, Gunn felt a little more at ease as he squared up to his opponent.

The two rapiers flashed in the air, clicking together momentarily in a gesture of sportsmanship. Gesture only, for a split second later, Gunn had to jump back hurriedly as Don Santoz flicked the wicked blade in a savage downward cut across his chest. Had the tip of the rapier found contact, it would have laid his flesh open from shoulder to stomach. Don Santoz pressed his early initiative with the skill of a master swordsman. As Gunn fell back, the Spaniard adjusted his feet to take up the gap and jabbed his sword forward in three smooth movements. Gunn felt the last thrust barely pluck against his belt, even as he drew back and gave more ground.

Don Santoz grunted with exertion as he pressed forward once again, curling the rapier in the air and making a downward thrust towards Gunn's arm. The tell-tale sign did not go unnoticed. Gunn's quiet confidence began to seep back again. That was the way then: to give ground, force Don Santoz to expend as much energy as possible. Make the older man tire himself, then take full advantage of his own youth and speed.

Acting upon his thoughts, Gunn left his body in a vulnerable position just long enough to tempt his opponent into movement. Santoz jumped forwards, lifting the rapier high in the air and bringing the flashing blade down in a sweeping arc. Gunn's timing was perfect. As the slash built up full inertia, he stepped effortlessly back on to the balls of his feet and watched the weight and momentum of the heavy steel take its toll on the Spaniard's muscles.

For a split second, Gunn nearly took advantage of Santoz' own position of open vulnerability, Like a reflex action, Gunn was instinctive to see that the man was off balance and unprotected. The sword in his hand seemed to have a life of its own, its sharp point questing eagerly for the taste of fresh, warm blood. Just in time, Gunn realised what was happening and pulled himself up. The automatic lunge forward was halted, his rapier barely missing its fleshy target in the Spaniard's stomach and merely slashing a foot-long passage through the material of his shirt.

Don Santoz seemed to realise that the near miss was a deliberate one. For the first time, his eyes showed a flash of doubt, a troubled mind. Then, driven by the heat of battle, it was gone again, to be replaced by the cold and ruthless gaze of a man driven to win. With renewed vigour, he set up another smooth series of attacking movements, the blade swinging through the air with deceptive laziness. Gunn, caught unawares, moved a little too slowly. A sharp stinging pain in his shoulder told him that the tip of Don Santoz' rapier had tasted first blood. He fell back quickly, gaining space and time to cast a quick glance down at the wound. It was little more than a deep scratch. He had been lucky. Gunn's eyes met those of his opponent, posing a silent question. It was met with a cold, impersonal gaze which carried its own answer. First blood would not be enough to satisfy honour and end the duel. The battle was to the death, as far as Don Santoz was concerned.

The Spaniard moved in again, lusting for the kill. The sense, however false, of any degree of sportsmanship was gone now. In its place, just the ruthless savagery of the predator closing upon its wounded victim. With a new lease of life and energy, Don Santoz seemed to shrug off his years and become an automatic, thoroughly efficient fighting machine. His thrusts and cuts were flawless, smooth in their execution and deadly in accuracy. Twice more, Gunn felt the faintest prick of steel as his opponent's rapier slashed through his clothing and found the flesh underneath. Blood bubbled out on his shoulder from a second wound, curling down his arm to make the hilt of the weapon warm and sticky in his grasp. Another scratch on his chest oozed enough blood to spread a crimson stain across his tattered shirt.

With a horrible feeling deep in the pit of his stomach, Gunn realised that he was tasting the bitter acid of defeat for the first time in his life. His throat tightened with it, his mouth drying up. His eyes were riveted upon the flashing silver of his opponent's weapon. Hypnotised, like a helpless rodent cornered by a snake, he could only make purely instinctive movements of self-preservation, his subconscious fully aware that it was now only a matter of time.

Perhaps, had Gunn's full concentration still been upon the swordplay, his eyes might have missed the brief flicker of movement behind the rocks to his right-hand side. Had he done so, the Santoz blood-line would certainly have come to an end that day.

From behind the cover of the surrounding boulders, the first bandit appeared, pistol in hand. Don Santoz' two guards, caught off guard, were not quick enough to save their lives. Two shots cracked out, each bullet finding a target. The two guards dropped, clutching at their chests in an ineffectual attempt to stem the flow of their life-blood.

'Look out.' Gunn's voice screamed out the warning just as the bandit turned his attention on the Spaniard. As he levelled his pistol at Don Santoz' back, Gunn's palm tightened around the hilt of the rapier and his arm came up and around in a wild swing. With all his might, he hurled the heavy sword through the air. Wild though it was, the hasty throw was accurate enough. The weapon cleaved through the air, point first towards the Mexican bandit's belly. He screamed horribly as it struck home, entering into the soft part of his belly just below the ribcage. The pistol dropped from his fingers into the sand as his dark eyes rolled in disbelief, then glazed over. Both hands contracted over the razor-sharp blade, the bandit buckled at the knees and toppled forward. The weight of his body pushed the scarlet-stained rapier right through his unresisting belly and out through his back. Completely impaled, the bandit convulsed upon the ground a couple of times, then lay still.

As he fell, Gunn was already running at a crouch towards the nearest of the dead guards. Throwing his body into a low, graceful dive, he hit the ground and took what cover he could behind the corpse, his hand clawing towards the man's holster. The big Smith and Wesson felt heavy and clumsy in his grasp, but it would serve its purpose well enough. Two more bandits showed themselves, stepping out into the open to get a clear shot at the unprotected Don Santoz. Gunn aimed quickly and squeezed the trigger twice in a row. The first slug ripped into the bandit's shoulder, pitching him round in a spin. The second bullet disposed of the second bandit cleanly and neatly, drilling a small hole in the very centre of his swarthy forehead. The Smith and Wesson barked a third time as the wounded man tried to crawl towards his gun. The bullet chewed deep into the base of his spine, bringing all movement and life to a sudden and complete stop.

Ready for more, Gunn's eyes flickered all over the surrounding rocks, but no more bandits appeared. Instead, there came the frantic whinnying of a horse being panicked into sudden movement, closely followed by the urgent pounding of hooves upon sand. The last bandit was taking no chances with his miserable skin. He had no wish to follow his companions to early graves.

Gunn raised the Smith and Wesson to take aim, then changed his mind upon a sudden impulse. This one, he wanted alive. Tucking the gun into his trousers, he turned and sprinted for his horse, urging it into a fast gallop before his feet were even snugly in the stirrups. The horse responded obediently, head down and mane flowing as it set out in chase.

The Mexican had over fifty yards start, but his underfed and water-rationed pony was no match for Gunn's steed. In seconds, the gap had narrowed to a matter of feet. The fleeing Mexican glanced over his shoulder in terror, then drew a pistol and hopelessly emptied it towards his pursuer. He might have just caught Gunn with a lucky shot, but his gods were not with him that day.

Gunn's hand snaked down to the smooth black handle of his bullwhip, sliding the coiled leather free from its special pommel-holster and flicking it out straight in the air behind him. Raising his arm, he flexed his muscles expertly, and with no more than an action from the wrist, sent the stinging end of the lash straight and true towards its target. The knotted end found its mark around the Mexican's neck, wrapping itself into a firm noose. Gunn braced himself in the saddle and pulled back his horse. The Mexican seemed to jump bodily backwards from his saddle as his mount continued its headlong flight out across the desert. He landed heavily, in a cloud of fine dust.

Gunn reined in his horse and threw himself down from the saddle to stand over the fallen bandit. The man was still, all the breath knocked from his body. There was no fight in him. Still, to be safe, Gunn took the precaution of bending down and quickly snatching the wicked-looking Apache scalping knife which the Mexican wore in his belt.

Pulling gently but firmly on the bullwhip, Gunn urged the fallen man to struggle to his feet. Uncoiling the whip, he flicked it a couple of times across the bandit's thighs. The stinging blows served their purpose to guide the Mexican in the direction Gunn wanted him to take. With no attempt at protest, he shambled across the desert back towards Don Santoz.

The Spaniard was badly shaken, but unhurt. His eyes held a strange mixture of guilt and gratitude as Gunn dismounted beside him. 'I owe you my life yet again, Señor Gunn,' he murmured in a broken voice. 'And my apologies, for ever doubting your word as a gentleman.'

'Forget it.' Gunn's voice was curt not out of rudeness but because there were far more urgent and important matters to be attended to. He flicked the whip lightly across his prisoner's back, but the pain of the lash was enough to cause a shrill cry of agony. 'Ask him what's going on,' he barked to Don Santoz.

The nobleman gabbled in his native tongue. The bandit, his eyes narrowed to slits, set his jaw in a firm line and refused to speak. Gunn cracked the lash twice more, stinging the Mexican once on his legs and once between the shoulder-blades. The double ration of pain was enough to loosen his stubborn tongue. He broke into a hurried gabble of words.

Although Gunn could not understand them, the look on Don Santoz' face alone was enough to tell him that it was grave news indeed. For the first time, Gunn saw pure, unashamed fear in the proud nobleman's eyes. Knowing the man as he had come to do, Gunn sensed instinctively that it was not his own life Don Santoz feared for.

His face ashen and trembling, Don Santoz turned back to Gunn as he translated the gist of the message. 'Estuarti has taken the main band of his bandidos to attack the hacienda. They intend to kidnap Rosita, then violate her to bring final dishonour upon the Santoz name.'

Gunn reached out to grasp the trembling nobleman by the shoulder. 'Quickly, Don Santoz. We may still be in time,' he urged.

Don Santoz shrugged away from the reassuring grip. His face was set and grim as he looked at the Mexican prisoner with loathing. His lips quivered as he hissed in a low voice. 'Kill this vermin, *Señor* Gunn.' He glanced down at the Smith and Wesson still in Gunn's hand.

Gunn's face clouded over. 'I can't do that, Don Santoz,' he murmured in return. He sheathed the gun. 'Come, there are more important things to worry about now.'

Don Santoz' voice rose to a tortured scream. 'Kill him, please.'

Gunn shook his head firmly before mounting his horse. He had no real part in the family drama which he had become involved in. It had brought him to kill again, but it would not bring him to cold-blooded murder.

Don Santoz seemed to understand. His head dropped on his shoulders. Still broken and trembling, he reached for the reins of his own horse and mounted up. As he seated himself in the saddle, it seemed that a sudden answer had come to him. Just for a moment, despite his grief and fear, a flash of pride lit up his face and his lips curled in a sneering smile. Before Gun realised what he was going to do, Don Santoz jabbed his spurred boots deep in to his mount's flanks and hauled back on the reins, letting out a high pitched yell at the same time. The horse reared in the air, its front hooves flashing.

Under Don Santoz' expert horsemanship, the bandit never had a chance. The rearing horse closed upon him, the deadly hooves raining down death-dealing blows upon his head and shoulders. His skull cracked open like a rotten walnut, the luckless Mexican fell to the sand where Don Santoz urged his horse to complete the job it had been forced to start. Gunn looked away in revulsion as Don Santoz deliberately trampled the body of the Mexican into a bloody and misshapen mass. Only when he had expended all his fury did the proud Spaniard turn his horse away and urge it towards the hacienda at a fast gallop.

Gunn spurred his own horse, falling into step beside Don Santoz. As they sped back towards the ranch, both men could hear the crackle of gunfire drifting across the desert. There was smoke rising into the cloudless sky. It seemed that there would be little left of the Santoz hacienda by the time they arrived back.

Chapter Nine

The scene of devastation and slaughter was as bad as Gunn had pictured in his mind. Once again, the courtyard of the hacienda was littered with bodies, and the groans of the wounded and dying filled the air. Most of the ranch outbuildings had been set afire, and were blazing uncontrollably. Even had there been spare hands to fetch and carry water, there would have been little hope of saving much. The hacienda itself bore more than its fair share of the scars of battle. Not a single window remained intact, bodies lay slumped against its walls, their blood splashed on the white stone and already beginning to dry a muddy brown under the blazing sun. The wooden porch had been fired, and although the blaze had been extinguished, little remained of the verandah except blackened stumps of the upright posts and the crumbling ashes of the floor boarding.

Don Santoz galloped straight through the smoke-filled courtyard to the front of the hacienda. Leaping from his saddle before the horse even came to a stop, he threw himself into the building, screaming his daughter's name.

When he emerged, a few moments later, he was utterly broken and distraught. Gunn knew, then, that the bandits had succeeded in their objective.

'Rosita?' he asked, gently, running to the nobleman's side.

With blank eyes, Don Santoz stared at him without seeing. His normally proud head nodded in dejection.

'Gone,' he muttered simply, in a quavering voice.

'Your wife?'

'Alive,' Don Santoz croaked. 'The animals spared her, at least.' He fell silent, his lips moving faintly as his unseeing eyes looked up towards the heavens. Gunn turned and walked away a discreet distance, leaving the man to conduct his prayers in privacy. He looked around the courtyard, counting and identifying the bodies. Most were Santoz' own men, but it was obvious that they had not let the hacienda fall easily. Gunn totted up over a score of dead bandits laying in the open, and guessed that there would be many more inside the hacienda itself. With no quarter given or expected, the last of the guards would have fought bravely for their lives.

He stooped over one wounded guard, who was groaning dully. A quick inspection of the man's wounds told Gunn that he did not have long to suffer. Three bullets had found their way into his body, and although no vital organs had been hit, the man lay in a thickening pool of blood. He had bled too much for too long to stand the faintest chance of survival. Gunn knelt, pressing his lips to the dying man's ear.

'Cuanto bandidos?' he whispered, hoping the man could understand his miserable attempt at pidgin Spanish.

The man's eyelids fluttered, his slack mouth barely moving. *'Ocho, señor.'* He struggled to sit up, but the effort finished him. His eyes glazed over, his body went slack. With a last, convulsive shudder, he made the transition into the after life.

Gunn straightened, slowly. So there were only eight members of the bandit gang still surviving! They had indeed paid dearly for Gomez Estuarti's insane desire to pursue his blood feud. Gunn turned his back on the dead guard, savouring the fact. It still did not sound too hopeful, since it appeared that no more than a handful of Don Santoz' men were left without serious wounds. On the other hand, it was better odds than he had secretly expected. It left he and Don Santoz with the faint chance of rescuing Rosita before she suffered the terrible fate Gomez Estuarti had planned for her.

From one of the blazing barns, a horrible, curdling scream snapped Gunn out of his thoughts. From the very midst of the flames ran a man – or what the fire had left of a man. His tattered clothing enveloped in flames, the tortured body of a bandit stumbled out into the open courtyard, arms flailing uselessly. A deep red furrow across his forehead showed where a bullet had creased his temple, obviously stunning him and leaving him unconscious while the fire spread all about him. The agony of the searing flames and heat had driven his mind back to the terrible effort of survival. It could be only a lost cause. The man's face was streaked with blood, his eyes blinded with that and the choking, swirling black smoke which had enveloped him. Where his flesh showed through the smoking tatters of his clothing, it bore ugly marks of terrible burns. A human pyre, it was only the blind animal instinct to fight against the certainty of death which made him move.

Horrified but fascinated, Gunn watched the terrible sight stumble across the courtyard. Kneeling in prayer, Don Santoz looked up and saw it too – and a split second before Gunn also saw the knife that the Mexican clutched in his fire-mutilated hand.

The burning man seemed to throw himself the last few feet towards his intended victim with almost supernatural effort. Gunn saw the knife's blade flash in the sunlight and clawed for the Smith and Wesson tucked into his trousers. He drew and fired too late to stop the weapon from being plunged deep into the nobleman's back.

The heavy Smith and Wesson bucked in Gunn's hand. The slug ploughed into the Mexican's chest, slamming him a good two feet clear of Don Santoz' slumped body. Gunn ran across to check his host's wound, wrinkling his nostrils in revulsion as the acrid smell of burned flesh filled them.

Don Santoz looked up at him, his eyes filled with physical pain heaped on top of the mental anguish he had already suffered. Gunn's keen eyes looked at the stab wound. It was deep, but hopefully not serious. The blade had penetrated several inches into the soft flesh of the Spaniard's left shoulder, but miraculously had not managed to sever a major blood vessel. Gunn bent over Don Santoz, helping him to his feet. He supported him under his good arm and led him across the courtyard towards the hacienda.

It was the first time Gunn had seen what the bandits had done to the interior of the beautiful Santoz home. The place was a shambles – a mute testimony to mindless violence and savage vandalism at its very worst. The rich fabrics of the curtains and upholstery had been slashed to tatters, the polished surfaces of the fine woodwork scarred beyond redemption with knives and flying bullets. Anything breakable in the hacienda had been thrown to the floors and trampled under heavy boots. Precious porcelain, delicate glassware, irreplaceable family heirlooms and portraits of Don Santoz' antecedents had not escaped the destruction. Gunn could quite understand why Don Santoz referred to the bandit horde as mere animals. Even some of the lower species would have some regard for another creature's abode.

The Spaniard's wife rushed to his side as Gunn dragged the wounded man inside. Despite all her grief, she rallied herself together to concentrate all her attention and sympathy upon him. Gunn left Don Santoz in her expert care and walked outside again to concentrate his thoughts.

They were not happy ones. No optimism on earth could make any difference to the harsh fact that he was now utterly alone, and the only person who could rescue Rosita. One man – with eight murderous and cut-throat bandits against him.

A lesser man might well have been forgiven had he saddled up and ridden away from the tail-end of a fight which was not his. Gunn stared at the empty corral where the black stallions had been kept, the faintest niggling doubts pricking at the back of his mind. Now that the horses were gone, the feud seemed all that much more pointless. Then the image of Rosita came to him clearly – screaming and struggling as eight filthy bandits tore at her fine clothing, their rough hands itching to claw the smoothness of her flesh. In an instant all doubts were gone. Gunn knew that he really had no choice. Whatever the circumstances, he must go to her aid.

The moment of final decision accelerated his movements. At a run, Gunn headed for the hacienda and went straight to his room. He tossed the Smith and Wesson on to the bed and hitched on his own gunbelt, checking each ivory-handled Colt and filling his pockets with plenty of spare ammunition.

Outside again, he mounted up and guided his horse out around the smouldering outbuildings to pick up the bandit gang's trail. It was plain enough. Thinking that they had wiped out all opposition, they had made no attempts to cover up their tracks. The trail led straight into the hills.

Gunn urged his horse forward at a moderate trot. Stealth would be more useful than speed, he figured. Rosita was unlikely to suffer her planned fate before nightfall, and the bandits themselves would not be in any great hurry. On top of which, Gunn fully realised that a reasonably fresh horse might well be his last resort when it came to saving his skin.

A half an hour's ride brought him to the lower foothills. Here the trail was not quite so obvious, but easy enough to pick out. It was not easy to take eight riders and a whole bunch of loose horses up a narrow mountain path without leaving plenty of marks in passing.

As he climbed, the path became increasingly steep. Gunn reined in his horse and dismounted, preferring to walk. He could make almost as much headway on foot as in the saddle, and freed of its rider's weight, the horse

76

made less sound upon the rocks to echo ahead through the hills and advertise its coming.

As it turned out, Gunn need not have worried about betraying himself with noise. It was the bandits themselves who announced their position long before he could have been within earshot. In the distance, a volley of gunshots cracked into the quiet air, rolling around between the sloping hills like thunder. Gunn stopped, pricking his ears. The ragged gunfire continued for several minutes, when it finally died away, Gunn could faintly hear the sounds of laughter and celebration.

He moved ahead with greater confidence, knowing that their racket would deafen them to the sound of his approach. Another ten minutes of climbing brought Gunn to the crest of the first range of hills. Rounding a huge clump of boulders, he could see for a couple of miles across the intervening valley ahead.

Two miles was more than enough. The bandit camp was less than a quarter of that distance away. Crouching behind the rocks just to be on the safe side, Gunn trained his keen eyes upon the scene.

The bandits were celebrating sure enough. Flushed with victory and convinced that they had left no survivors, they were letting themselves go. Whooping and shouting, they ran wildly through the roughly circular camp congratulating themselves upon their victory and its spoils. Gunn's face broke into a grim smile as he saw that each man held a bottle of whisky or tequila in his hand. He tethered his horse to a gnarled tree-stump and sat down in the shade of a large rock to wait. He closed his eyes against the brightness of the overhead sun, confident that the passage of time could now only help him more and more. Left alone, the bandits would get drunk soon enough, and the fierce heat of the sun would soon put them in the mood for a siesta. It would make things a whole lot easier, Gunn reflected, with more optimism than he had felt for a long while.

Two hours passed. Only when the faint sounds of laughter had faded did Gunn open his eyes and push

himself to his feet. He peered out once again from behind the rock.

The camp was quiet now, and nothing moved. Just as
he had expected, the bandits had drunk themselves into
a stupor and were now sleeping it off. Only the horses
moved restlessly, uncomfortable in the heat of the afternoon sun.

Gunn gave them another half an hour to settle happily
into their dreams before making a move. Still pulling
his horse behind him, he began to skirt carefully around
the rim of the valley looking for the shortest and easiest
route down.

There seemed to be only one – the trail the bandits
had taken. It was a steep, straight path down through
the rocks and into the valley, but the ground was
covered in loose shale which would slither and rattle
underfoot. There seemed no way of getting down into
the camp quietly. Gunn stopped, looking around carefully. To attempt to go down the obvious trail was court-
ing suicide. There was no way he could get anywhere
near the sleeping bandits without arousing them. Once
that happened, he would be a sitting target for eight
guns.

There *was* another way! It was risky, but Gunn felt
that he had no choice. The only way to get into the
bandit camp quietly was straight down. Gunn quietly
uncoiled a long rope from his saddle and slung it over
his broad shoulders. Carefully, he scrambled down the
rocks on his bottom, letting only the soft leather sides
of his boots scrape against the boulders.

He came to a large, flat rock which overlooked the
valley. From there, it was a fifty foot drop straight down
to the outer perimeter of the camp. It was the only
chance. Gunn unwound the rope, fashioned a strong
noose at one end and fastening it securely around the
lip of the overhanging rock. Gently he lowered down the
remainder of the rope until it dangled, just a few feet
above the valley floor. Taking a firm grip, he slid to the
very edge and launched himself into space.

His arms strained to endurance, Gunn inched slowly down the rope until he came to the end of it. He glanced down. His feet were no more than three feet from the ground. He dropped gently, landing lightly on his feet. Gunn's heart was pounding in his chest as he looked around the bandit encampment. All seemed quiet enough. Gunn picked out four of the bandits, sprawled out in small patches of shade in their drunken sleep. Of the rest, and Rosita, there was no sign. Gunn could only surmise that she was held prisoner in one of the half-dozen tents which dotted the camp. No doubt they also housed the remainder of the gang and Estuarti himself.

With cold-blooded efficiency, Gunn selected his first victim. He could not afford to let finer principles affect him. It was a simple case of kill or be killed. The quieter and the quicker he could accomplish that killing, so much the better for him.

He crept stealthily towards the nearest sleeping Mexican, pulling his Bowie knife from his belt as he moved. The bandit dozed on, oblivious to the death which approached him. He was snoring deeply, not moving except for the steady rising and falling of his barrel-like chest.

The sound of his snoring ceased abruptly as Gunn's palm clamped over his nose and mouth. The rise and fall of his chest ceased a split second afterwards, when Gunn plunged the sharp blade deep into his heart. The Mexican died without a sound to betray the presence of his killer within the camp.

His nearest companion also died silently, the keen edge of the knife slicing through his windpipe and vocal cords as Gunn attacked him from behind. Gunn wiped the blood off the blade on his trousers, putting the hilt of the knife between his teeth as he tried to do the same for his hands. They were warm and sticky with the blood which had gushed from his victim's jugular vein. It was an unpleasant feeling, and Gunn knew he would need his fingers dry and clean when the inevitable gunplay started.

It was nearer than he had supposed. A few yards in front of him, one of the sleeping bandits stirred, rolled over and knocked his head lightly against a loose rock. The sudden pain of it was enough to shake him rudely awake, his eyes unluckily aimed in Gunn's direction.

As the Mexican screamed a warning, and his hand clawed for his pistol, Gunn's hands flashed to his holster. He drew both Colts simultaneously, aiming and firing as soon as they came clear of leather. The Mexican's return to the world of the awake and living was a short trip. With the yell of alarm still on his lips, he fell back into an eternal sleep as a heavy .45 slug chewed into his temple. The fourth bandit had just time enough to reach his gun and loose off one wild shot before two bullets found their resting place in his stomach and chest. Sober and alert, he might have had a chance to save his life. Waking suddenly, with the sun in his eyes and tequila fumes clouding his brain, he had no chance at all. His one bullet whistled harmlessly through the air, a good four feet away from Gunn's body.

Gunn dived to the ground, his arms outstretched and his fingers still curled purposefully around the triggers of the Colts. His keen eyes took in the whole camp area at once, paying particular attention to the tents.

It was a wise precaution. From one of them, two bandits darted out, pistols in hand. They never saw a target to aim them at. Gunn's right-hand Colt barked three times, two of the bullets striking home. The two bandits dropped a few feet outside their tent without ever having known from which direction the killer bullets had come.

Six down. Two to go then, Gunn's racing brain reminded him. Suddenly it was only one, as a bullet slammed into the sand beside him and a blur of movement caught the corner of his eyes. To his right. Gunn rolled over quickly, bringing his hand up and firing on the rise. The seventh bandit, who had obviously been sleeping behind the shade of the rocks screamed and threw up his hands as the slug blasted its way through his ribcage and deflected across his heart.

'James.' The shrill scream rang out across the Valley, echoing back from the surrounding hills.

It was Rosita's voice. Gunn whirled in the direction from which it had come, starting to scramble to his feet. She was framed in the open front of the largest tent. She was not alone. Shielded behind her body stood a young Mexican. His arm was firmly around her throat. His free hand held a pistol, which was firmly pressed against the side of her head.

'Drop your gun, or she dies, Gringo.'

Gunn's fingers only tightened around the trigger. 'Estuarti?' he called, uncertainly.

Si,' the young Mexican replied with a nod. 'You are *Señor* Gunn, no?'

'That's right. We have no real quarrel, Estuarti. Your feud is with Don Santoz. Let the girl go, and I have no reason to kill you.'

The Mexican's face seemed to screw up with anger at the name. 'Don Santoz lives?'

Gunn nodded. 'He lives.'

Estuarti let loose a string of obscenities in his native tongue. Falling silent for a few seconds, he glanced around the camp at the bodies of his companions. He let out a bitter laugh. 'You say we have no quarrel, *Señor* Gunn – yet you have killed all my men.'

Gunn's voice was firm and controlled. 'Your finger was also upon the trigger, Estuarti. They died fighting for your personal blood feud which should have been over years ago.'

Gunn's words carried the chilling ring of truth. Gomez Estuarti's face creased into thoughtful reverie for a while. Finally he nodded. 'It is as you say, *Señor* Gunn. Too much innocent blood has been shed. The matter remains between Don Santoz and myself, as it has always been.'

'Let Rosita go,' Gunn prompted gently.

The Mexican hesitated, but the gun no longer pressed against his victim's temple quite so firmly. His arms

6   81

relaxed around her throat, but he was still not quite convinced. 'I could kill her now,' he murmured, distantly. 'Another Santoz wiped from the face of the earth.'

'And the last of the Estuarti's right alongside her,' Gunn countered. 'You die the second any harm comes to her.'

There were a few moments of terrible tension as Estuarti considered the possibilities. At last, to Gunn's relief, it broke. Estuarti lowered the pistol and dropped it to the ground. He removed his arm from around Rosita's throat and pushed her gently in the back. With a strangled cry of relief, she ran from him to Gunn's side. clinging on his arm and sobbing heavily.

Gunn looked at the young Mexican squarely. Slowly, he sheathed his Colt, throwing his arm around the girl's heaving shoulders. 'Are you all right?' he whispered down to her.

Rosita choked back her tears and forced a nod. 'I am all right now,' she murmured. 'I feared you would all be dead. He told me that my father had been killed and hung from the hacienda porch.'

'No, your father is fine,' Gunn reassured her, conveniently leaving out the fact that he had been wounded.

Taking his eyes off the young Mexican for the first time, Gunn steered Rosita gently around in a half-circle. 'Let's get home now,' he said quietly.

They started to walk away. Behind them, Estuarti's voice barked out suddenly. '*Señor* Gunn?'

Gunn turned, half expecting to face a pistol once again. He was wrong Estuarti had made no attempt to pick up his discarded weapon. He stood, arms akimbo, regarding them cooly.

'Yes?' Gunn said, quietly.

'I wish to ride back with you – to the hacienda,' Estuarti said in a quiet, but firm voice. 'It is as you said – the time has come for this feud of blood to be finished.'

Gunn nodded, understanding. 'As you wish, Estuarti.' He turned back towards the black stallions for a second, gesturing towards them. 'You will bring the horses?'

Estuarti nodded. '*Si*. I will bring the horses.'

Satisfied with the man's word, Gunn turned his back on him once again and led Rosita away from the scene of slaughter. He lifted her up on to the back of his horse before mounting up himself. Behind them, Estuarti gathered the stallions together on a long leading rein and mounted his own pinto.

In a slow procession, the riders and spare horses headed back towards the Santoz ranch.

Chapter Ten

The two old enemies faced each other with undisguised loathing and hostility. The hatred, fed by the past generations through the years, was a tangible force which seemed to fill the room and pervade the entire Santoz hacienda. It was all Gunn could do to stop the two men from flying at each others throats. He trod his ground warily, between the wounded but fiercely active Don Santoz and the young Gomez. More than once he had to lay a restraining hand against the Spanish nobleman's chest as he struggled to rise from his chair and fly at his adversary. Gomez himself seemed only slightly more relaxed, yet the tortured twitching of his facial muscles betrayed some of his thoughts.

Gunn felt overpowered by it all. He had never before in his life faced such utterly blind and unreasonable hate. Had he ever really seriously considered guiding the two men to a truce, he forgot any such idea now. There could never be any give in either man. Their fierce family pride, and the hot blood of their race, made them blaze at each other with raw, negative energy. Like two like magnetic poles, it radiated out in a field which affected everything within it.

He had tried, of course. Sending Rosita and her mother away, Gunn had tactfully engineered the situation, bringing the two men face to face for the first time. He had hoped that the sheer savagery of the slaughter over the last few days would have chilled them, dampened down the flames of the feud, but it was no use. Still, Gunn was unwilling to be beaten. He tried once more.

'There is an honourable way out of this – for both of you,' he said with grim determination. 'Divide the herd – let Gomez take half the horses and pasture them somewhere on your vast lands.'

His words ran off Don Santoz like water off a duck's back. The man gritted his teeth, hissing through them with all the venom of a rattlesnake. 'No.'

Gunn realised, then, that it wasn't really the horses. Not any more. Perhaps they had never really mattered – except once, for a brief while long ago. The black stallions were only a symbol of the family feud, they were no longer important in themselves. The real hatred was deeper, born in each new member of both families like a physical characteristic, and fed and nurtured in them from the womb to the grave. Gunn recognised all this, although he did not fully understand it. Perhaps the English mentality never could grasp such a powerful, yet abstract concept. Family pride he knew about, but it would have been tempered and softened by a fraction of the massacres and bloodshed which had divided the Santoz and Estuarti families over the years.

Gunn felt weary with the hopelessness of the situation. The two men's hatred had drained him. His shoulders slumped with resignation. There was nothing more he could do. There could never be any peace while both men lived. Peace could only come with death. It was clear and inevitable.

Gomez Estuarti summed it up. He spoke in a quiet, almost detached voice. 'There is only one way this feud of blood can end,' he murmured softly, to no one in particular. 'It will be as it must be – as the fates have decreed it would be.' He pulled himself erect, turning to face Don Santoz directly. His young face was pulled into a proud, defiant mask. 'I will go now, Don Santoz, but I will return in four days, when your wound is better. You will honour and avenge my forbearers then, with the duel.'

Don Santoz also pulled himself together, switching off the loathing and raw hate for long enough to maintain an air of quiet dignity. 'It shall be so, Gomez Estuarti,' he replied. 'But it is my forbearers who shall be appeased, by your blood upon the sand.'

Gomez nodded his head, briefly, and spun on his heels. Without another word, he strode briskly to the door and walked out.

As the door closed behind him, Don Santoz seemed to fold up and collapse across his desk like a limp rag doll. His rage and blazing hatred had sustained him for the past few minutes as an energy force. Now he was morally and physically drained. Weak from loss of blood and the hectic events of the past few days, he could no longer maintain the illusion of strength and determination.

Gunn looked at him pityingly for a few moments. Then, satisfied that the man was sleeping, he left the room quietly to find Rosita and her mother.

They accepted the news with philosophical calmness. It was, after all, exactly what they had expected and prepared themselves for. The feud was somehow in their blood too, like an insidious poison which could be transmitted through thought, or close contact over many years. Neither woman allowed herself to cry, although their faces tautened. Don Santoz' wife laid her arm around Rosita's shoulder. 'Come, daughter, we shall go and pray to the Blessed Mother,' she said quietly.

The four days dragged by like an eternity. Don Santoz spent most of his time alone, either resting in bed to recover his strength, or locked in his study. At meal times, either Rosita or his wife would prepare him a private tray and serve it in his room. On the odd occasions when he bumped into Gunn, there was no attempt at conversation. Don Santoz was a man alone, his concentration exclusively fixed upon the coming showdown.

Several times, Gunn considered leaving. Life in the hacienda was cold and impersonal. He felt almost unwanted, although Rosita still tried bravely to smile at him from time to time. But her thoughts too, were really elsewhere. Every time he thought about returning to the Cunningham ranch in California, Gunn realised that he was virtually trapped. He could not, in all conscience, go before the drama he had become involved in had been played out to its final scene. He had come so far with the Santoz family. Now he must see it through to the end. Besides, Gunn told himself, his presence as an impartial referee would be needed when the two men came to fight their duel. Afterwards, his presence as a man might be needed for other things – for Rosita was not close to her mother. She had always been her father's daughter – it was partly in the blood, partly the traditional Spanish way. Don Santoz had wanted a son, but he was man enough to hide any suggestion that he had ever felt that he had got second-best.

Gomez Estuarti kept his word. On the morning of the fourth day he arrived at the hacienda, alone and unarmed. He was strangely calm. He faced Don Santoz once again over the nobleman's desk. 'The time for final reckoning is come, Don Santoz,' he murmured quietly.

The man nodded. 'Let blood avenge honour,' he responded.

Estuarti inclined his head towards the bandage Don Santoz still wore around his left shoulder. 'Your wound is not yet quite healed,' he pointed out. 'I suggest, therefore, that we choose the pistols as our duelling weapon. It would be unfair of me to take advantage of you by choosing the rapiers.'

Don Santoz nodded in agreement. 'As you wish.' He turned to Gunn. '*Señor* Gunn would you be so good as to prime and load the weapons please. I will deem it a favour if you will conduct yourself as second for both of us.'

'Of course.' Gunn took the boxed pistols which Don Santoz handed to him and carefully loaded them with ball and powder. Satisfied that they were both ready to serve their destructive purpose, he replaced them in their case and snapped it shut.

Outside, the sun was fully risen, but the morning air was still cool. Estuarti glanced out of the window, nodding thoughtfully. 'It is not dignified for a man to have to die in the heat of the midday sun,' he muttered distantly. 'Can I suggest that we get this thing over with?'

'Let it be so,' Don Santoz responded politely. Now that the moment had come, both men seemed controlled and calm. The fierce hate seemed to have been washed away temporarily in the face of death. Perhaps both men partially realised that life, with its trivialities, paled into utter insignificance in the cold shadow of the grim reaper.

Gunn tucked the pistols under his arm and led the way silently into the courtyard. The two combatants stood squarely, facing each other. Reluctantly, Gunn opened the pistol box. 'I ask you both for the last time,' he pleaded. 'Forget this feud, bury the past once and forever and make your peace with yourselves and with God.'

Both men shook their proud heads stubbornly. Gunn had hardly expected any other reaction, not at this stage of the drama. 'Prepare yourselves then, gentlemen,' he said in a hushed voice.

Don Santoz turned away, knelt down and clasped his hands together in prayer. Estuarti contented himself with merely raising his eyes to Heaven and murmuring under his breath. Gunn found it more than slightly ironic that both men were praying in the name of the Prince of Peace for the good fortune to kill each other.

The prayers were brief. Don Santoz regained his feet, standing stiffly and proudly as Gunn displayed the open pistol box between him and his opponent. Each man took a weapon, balancing it in their hands to get the weight and feel of it.

Gunn gave them their last-minute instructions, even though both men knew what was expected of them. 'You will stand back to back,' Gunn said solemnly.

'When I start to count, you will each walk ten paces, turn and fire at will.' He paused. 'Understood?'

Both men nodded. They turned slowly, their backs just touching. When next they were face to face, death would be only a split second away for one of them. The large lead balls used in the pistols made virtually sure that almost any hit was as good as a kill. It was highly unlikely that either man could miss at the range.

'One,' Gunn intoned grimly, 'two, three, four.'

In perfect step, the two duellists took their careful measured paces across the sun-baked earth. From the corner of his eye, Gunn saw that Rosita and her mother had ventured out on to the charred ruins of the porch to watch. Gunn hoped they would not have to see their man die.

'Five, six, seven, eight.'

The two men walked stiffly, jerkily – strangely like pall-bearers at a funeral, Gunn mused idly. To all aspects of death, there seemed to be a ritual.

'Nine, ten.'

Gunn's breath caught in his throat as he counted off the tenth and final pace. The two men froze momentarily, then both spun smoothly round on their toes, the pistols in their hands coming up in one straight, clean movement.

Estuarti's pistol discharged first, with a dull report. Gunn saw Don Santoz stiffen, the colour draining from his face. His pain-filled eyes barely flickered downwards, but they had time enough to see the scarlet rivulet running from his lower belly. With that sight came the certain knowledge of death.

There was a terrible silence. Even the faint breeze which had been blowing seemed to have did down as if in reverence for the gravity of the moment. Don Santoz was dying, a blood-feud which had persisted through many generations was finally coming to its end.

He was dying – but he had not yet discharged his pistol. Gomez Estuarti stared at his adversary with a strange mixture of emotions upon his face. Surprise that his shot had not taken the man down cleanly, pity that Don Santoz was surely dying in great agony, even a twinge of admiration for the raw guts of the man. It was as if he clung to life with some superhuman will, refusing to fall.

Don Santoz' eyes were misting over with pain. His knees trembled beneath him. Yet, still he managed to hold off death, stay on his feet. With slow, rather jerky movements, he brought up his pistol.

Gomez Estuarti knew at that moment that he too would die. In a way, he now saw that the anger of his ancestors had always decreed that it would be so. There was no fear in his eyes as he faced the man who would kill him. 'Shoot, Don Santoz. Quickly, before it is too late,' he whispered urgently. 'I am not afraid to die. We both die, purging this land of our guilt.'

He straightened himself, stiffening his body and holding his head high.

'It must be so,' Don Santoz croaked weakly as the blood bubbled up in his throat. His finger tightened upon the trigger of the duelling pistol. In the last instant before his death, his control was absolute. The shot was straight and true, the heavy ball taking Estuarti between the eyes.

The two men dropped together. Gunn watched them fall, then turned, slowly and sadly back towards the two women. Neither had screamed, but now they huddled together in their mutual sorrow, sobbing gently. Death was no surprise to them. They had lived in its shadow for all their lives. Without a word, they turned and walked into the hacienda together. There were things to attend to – important things. No Santoz had ever departed the world without ceremony. There was the laying out to arrange, the priest and mourners to summon. Genuine mourners would be difficult to find, but there were plenty available who would put up a good show for the right price. They wore their blacks as a cowboy wore his chaps – they were the costume of their profession.

Their tears and moans would pour for every peso which crossed their palms.

Gunn stared down at the two bodies once more, the heaviness in his heart beginning to lift now that it was irrevocably finished. Both men had made their choice voluntarily, yet both seemed to have realised the true futility of it all in the final moments. They had lived as enemies, filled with hate for one another. In death, they had seen each other as men of honour, bound by the same blind law which had blighted their birthrights. In Heaven, perhaps, they could make their peace with each other. Gunn was not normally a particularly fervent believer, but now he secretly hoped that this could be so. If there were no justice in this world, there surely ought to be in the next.

A week had passed. The funeral was over and Gunn was preparing to leave. Rosita and her mother had coped well, finding comfort in each other and seeking refuge in that strange inner peace which is peculiar to staunchly catholic peoples. Gunn had no worries about leaving them, now that it was all over.

Rosita even managed a weak smile as he prepared to mount up and ride away from the hacienda forever. 'Goodbye, James Gunn,' she murmured, only the faintest trace of sadness in her voice. 'Thank you for everything you did . . . and tried to do.'

Gunn smiled back, then turned to look at the two proud black stallions tethered behind his own horse. Rosita had insisted upon his taking them as a gift. 'My father would have wanted you to have them,' she had assured him. 'He died in your debt.'

Had it not been for John Cunningham's dream, Gunn would have discreetly refused the gift. The black stallions were still the symbol of all those years of bloodshed and blind stupidity. Had it been his choice, he would have forgotten the animals completely.

But the choice was not his. He had come to fetch back the horses, and he was bound to complete his mission.

91

He only prayed that the black stallions were washed now of the taint of blood which had cursed them.

Gunn mounted up, turning in the saddle to wave one last time at the two women. Then, without a word, he turned back and spurred his mount forward. He did not look back. There was a lot he wanted to forget before he got back to California.

Chapter Eleven

Gunn had expected to be greeted by John Cunningham's overjoyed face as he rode up to the porch of the Circle 8 ranch house. Instead, there was only Lydia, looking pale and distraught. She burst into tears as Gunn dismounted and ran to her side.

'Lydia. What is it, what's happened?'

The story came out between sobs. Piecing it together, Gunn felt a sense of disbelief, turning to anger when Lydia told him how the local townspeople had turned against her husband.

'Why they know better than to think for a second that John could be a horse-thief and a murderer,' he said explosively. 'Surely they'll come to their senses and realise that it's a frame-up when the case comes to trial.'

Lydia Cunningham collapsed into anguished sobs with renewed despair. 'The trial was three days ago,' she screamed. 'They found him guilty, James. Don't you realise? They've already set the hanging for the day after tomorrow.'

Gunn had been shocked before. Now he was utterly stunned. 'Hanging?' he managed to breathe querulously.

Lydia Cunningham drew herself up with a deep breath, fighting for self-control. Gunn had to admire her. She nodded curtly, choking back her tears. 'That's right. We've got to do something, James.'

Gunn threw his arm reassuringly around her slim shoulders. 'I'll do something, don't you worry,' he promised. 'I'll get it all sorted out.'

He forced a mischievous grin. 'I'll have John back

here busting broncos in no time at all.'

The smile didn't really carry much weight, but Lydia blurted out a nervous laugh anyway, to show she appreciated the attempt. She was a brave woman, Gunn thought warmly. A good woman, who fully deserved the love of a good man like John Cunningham.

There was no time to lose. Gunn unhitched the two stallions and ushered them into the corral. Choosing a fresh horse, he changed over his saddle and mounted up again. Although he was weary from his long ride, he could not take time to rest. With a last, forced cheery wave to Lydia Cunningham, he rode at full gallop towards town.

Sheriff Baines glanced up from his desk as Gunn burst into his office without bothering to knock on the door. 'Something troubling you, Gunn?' he drawled sarcastically.

Gunn slammed his right fist upon the desk, his face twisted up in anger. 'Damn right there's something bothering me, Sheriff. And it ought to be bothering you too, knowing you got an innocent man in this jail waiting to hang for something he didn't do.'

There was no need to mention John Cunningham's name. Baines knew who Gunn was talking about. He pursed his lips, eyeing Gunn speculatively. 'Judge and jury said different, Gunn,' he pointed out. 'Cunningham got a fair trial. A damn sight fairer than many folks in this town woulda liked. Old Elmer was a popular old-timer round here. It was as much as I could do to stop a lynching, once folks found how he'd been gunned down in cold blood.'

'That was real nice of you, sheriff,' Gunn muttered sarcastically. 'Guess that makes for a nice, easy life, don't it? Seem a pity to waste your valuable time looking for a real killer running loose when you got a nice, convenient innocent man just sitting in your lap all nice and pat.'

'You're the only one who says he's innocent,' Baines retorted coldly. 'I just do my job, Gunn – and no matter what you think, it ain't an easy one.'

Gunn saw he could get nowhere pursuing the current line of conversation. He tried a different tack. His face softened slightly. 'OK, I'll concede that,' he admitted. 'But in all honesty, sheriff, don't you smell a rat somewhere? Surely you've known John Cunningham long enough to know what kind of a man he is.'

Sheriff Baines gave Gunn a cool appraising look. 'Yep, I know Cunningham well enough,' he murmured at last. 'But I don't know you too well, Gunn. What I *do* know is that you ain't exactly trigger-shy, and killing don't seem to come too hard to you. Truth of the matter is, it's only Cunningham's word that you were away in Mexico which clears you of this rap. Now if Cunningham's covering for you, and laying his own life on the line to do it, I'd say he is either an accesory to the murder or just a plain damned fool. Like you say, I should know Cunningham. I know for sure that he ain't no fool.'

'You accusing me, sheriff?' Gunn said quietly. His eyes blazed with a cold fire.

Baines ignored the direct question. Instead, he muttered: 'You seem all-fired convinced that John Cunningham is innocent. Could mean you know something I don't

It was pointless taking the conversation any further. With a weary sigh, Gunn gave up. 'Can I see the prisoner?'

Baines nodded. 'Take off your gunbelt first, Gunn.'

Gunn's fingers moved to his buckle. Baines spoke again. 'Just in case you got any crazy ideas, my deputy's got a scattergun trained on your guts from behind the door over there.' With a nod of his head, he gestured to the connecting door between the office and the cells behind.

'No ideas, Sheriff,' Gunn assured him coldly, slipping off his belt and laying it across the desk. 'Hoping to get some, though.'

The door creaked fully open. The deputy strolled into

the office, slipping the catch off the Starr .54 he cradled under his arm. 'OK to let him through now, sheriff?'

Baines nodded. 'Don't leave 'em alone though,' he warned. 'You listen to every word, you hear?'

'Got you, sheriff.' The deputy turned to Gunn. 'OK. Follow me.' He kicked open the door again, ushering Gunn through first. 'Third cell along,' he muttered, using the shotgun to point the way. 'And don't forget I'm right behind you, just like sheriff Baines said.'

'Let me in and you can peek through the keyhole,' Gunn said with bitter sarcasm. He walked along the corridor to the cell which housed John Cunningham.

Recognising him, the condemned man ran to the bars, a flash of hope on his troubled face for the first time in a week. 'Jim. Good to see you. Any news?'

Gunn shook his head sadly. 'What the hell is going on here?' he demanded.

Despite his predicament, Cunningham managed to grin weakly. 'Looks like I got myself into something of a mess,' he admitted sheepishly. 'I guess Lydia filled you in with the details, such as they are?'

Gunn nodded again. 'Sure. None of it makes any sense, though. You got any ideas? Any ideas at all?'

Cunningham looked down at the floor, shaking his head. 'Nothing, Jim. I've racked my brains time and time again, but I just can't figure out anything at all.'

'Well it's a frame, that's for sure,' Gunn murmured. 'But who, that's the question?'

Cunningham spread his hands in a hopeless gesture. 'Your guess is as good as mine, Jim.'

Gunn forced his mind to become cool and detached. Guesswork was not what was needed. It was time for logic, and a positive attitude to prevail. 'Look, John,' he asked after a few seconds of thought. 'Can you think of anyone who has a real bad grudge against you? Anyone who would profit from getting you out of the way?'

Cunningham shook his head. 'I ain't saying I'm the most popular man in America,' he murmured. 'But I

96

don't think I've made any real enemies in my time – specially not around these parts.'

The man whose horses were stolen. Sorenson. Any reason he might want to frame you? You're both in the same business. Could he want to be the unopposed local horse baron?'

Cunningham laughed. 'No way. I've known Lars Sorenson for years. Dammit, he's always been a good friend. We ain't in any real opposition. We do different kinds of business. No, you'll have to look elsewhere, Jim.'

'I intend to,' Gunn informed him firmly. 'If need be, I'll go right through this town with a fine toothcomb.'

'Got yourself a real job there, Mister Gunn,' the deputy sheriff drawled. 'Less than 24 hours to the hanging.'

Gunn fought to control his rage and frustration. For two pins, he would have turned and hit the man – shotgun or no shotgun. It was only the knowledge that such action could only doom John Cunningham even more which prevented him. He didn't bother to show the man his jibe had been heard, let alone registered. He kept his attention on Cunningham. 'Can't you think of anyone at all who might bear you a grudge – no matter how slight?'

'Ain't never knowingly cheated anybody, mind my own business most of the while. On good speaking terms with most folks in town – or at least I was, 'til this thing blew up. Nope, really Jim. I just can't think of a soul who'd want to cause trouble like this for me.'

Gunn stared into his frank, honest face. Cunningham was truthful enough with himself to know what he was talking about, he decided. That left him with absolutely no motive at all. There had to be a reason why Cunningham had been picked for such an obvious frame – unless there had been a terrible mistake somewhere. Suddenly, for the first time, a glimmering of the truth struck home. Inwardly, Gunn cursed himself for a fool for not having seen it at once. A tiny piece of the jigsaw slipped neatly into place.

Of course! Maybe John Cunningham had no enemies in Sagebrush Flats, but Gunn had. In this short time, he had managed very well to stir up envy, hatred . . . and fear. Any one of those emotions were enough to drive a certain type of man to seek a desperate way out. So that was it! It was himself who had been the intended victim. Something had gone wrong, and the blame had fallen upon John Cunningham in his place.

It didn't take Gunn long to figure out that the mistake must be something to do with his trip to Mexico. No one other than Cunningham would have known of his mission, or when he was to set out on it. He hadn't spent much time in Sagebrush Flats before his departure, so no one would have particularly noticed his absence, or given it any thought.

Once he had figured this much out, it didn't tax Gunn's brain unduly to identify the most likely suspects. Indeed, the more Gunn thought about it the Shobrook family became the *only* suspects.

Interrupting his thoughts, the deputy stepped forward and jabbed the twin barrels of the shotgun forward, smashing Cunningham's fingers against the metal bars of his cell. Incensed that Gunn had chosen to ignore his earlier jibe, he had found another way to take out his ill-feelings. 'OK visiting time's over,' he snapped curtly as Cunningham jumped back with a grunt of pain. The deputy turned to Gunn. 'You can see your buddy again, Gunn – dangling from the end of a rope.'

Once again, Gunn had to steel every nerve in his body to stop himself from smashing his fist into the deputy's evil, grinning face. Instead, he had to content himself with just a hissed threat. 'You're going to regret that.'

The deputy spat at his feet. 'You ain't gonna live long enough, Gunn,' he muttered venomously. 'Lotta folks in this town reckon you ought to be strung up alongside of Cunningham here. Sure reckon Sheriff Baines and

98

I ain't gonna put up too much of a fight when they get round to starting up another lynching party.'

This information came as a sobering warning to Gunn. He had not faced the possibility before. Now, thinking about it, he had to concede that the deputy probably had a point. There would be a lot of the towns-folk who would consider his supposed absence in Mexico a very thin alibi indeed. After all, they only had John Cunningham's word for it. And Cunningham was a convicted horse-thief and murderer. Gunn would have many more enemies in town now – and there would be no one willing to help him track down the truth. Indeed, he would probably meet with a great deal of active opposition. It was not a comforting realisation.

He smiled once at John Cunningham before turning to leave. 'Keep your chin up John. I'll have you out of there in no time at all.'

Cunningham made no reply. Nursing his bruised fingers, he had already slipped back into the despair which had haunted him for the past week. It was hard to seek hope when all logic told a man there was none to be found. Besides, outside in the town square, they had started to build the scaffold. The sound of the timbers being nailed into position filtered clearly down the street and in through the one small window of the jail cell. Come sundown, and Cunningham knew that he would be able to look out of that window and see the terrible, elongated shadow of the gibbet and noose stretched out along the main street.

Sheriff Baines looked up as Gunn walked back into his office. 'Guess you realise there's a lot of folks out there who would quite happily gun you down on the spot,' he said, echoing his deputy's warning.

Gunn nodded. 'Your little bully-boy here has already made quite a point of telling me.' He paused, to flash Baines an ironic smile. 'Guess that might suit you down to the ground, eh sheriff? Neatly remove any little loose ends that might otherwise trouble your conscience.'

Dunno what you're getting at, Gunn,' Baines grunted.

'Don't you?' Gunn regarded him with a questioning gaze. 'Things are pretty neat and bundled up at the moment, aren't they? Hang John Cunningham and you can sleep easy in your bed at nights, knowing full well he hasn't got any kin besides Lydia to come seeking vengeance.'

Baines glared nastily. 'Spit it out, Gunn. Say what's on your mind.'

'The Shobrook brothers. That's what's on my mind,' Gunn told him flatly. 'Seems to me you might have figured something out if you'd really tried, Baines. Also seems like you might not have wanted to.'

The barb struck home. Gunn saw the flash of shame which temporarily clouded the sheriff's eyes. 'Don't push your luck, Gunn,' he growled quietly but menacingly. 'I could impound your guns, you realise that?'

The threat failed to scare Gunn as it was meant to. Instead, he looked at the sheriff with pity. 'Guess there's quite a few things you *could* do, Baines . . . if you had the guts.'

He leaned over the desk and snatched up his gunbelt. Baines merely glared at him sullenly as he buckled it on and adjusted his thigh-cinches. Satisfied, he turned away and walked to the office door. 'Baine's voice snapped out uncertainly. 'What you planning on doing, Gunn?'

'Your job, maybe,' Gunn retorted, stepping out into the street and letting the door slam behind him.

He paused on the boardwalk, looking up and down the street. It was quiet. The gallows were rapidly taking shape, and its presence tended to keep people off the street. Any minute now would come the series of wooden crashes, swiftly followed by the swish of rope as the carpenters began testing the trap mechanism. It wasn't a sound ordinary folks cared to hear.

It was a good thing, Gunn thought to himself. The less people about to notice his presence in town the better. He had a lot to do, and very little time to do it in. Gunn could do without any harassment for the next few hours.

He walked under the shadow of the scaffold, steeling himself to repress a shudder. It didn't work. Quickening his pace, he crossed the square and discreetly ducked into the doorway of the barber shop. Glancing in through the window, Gunn saw it was empty. He opened the door quickly and briskly strode in.

'Be right with you,' called a voice from the room out back. A few seconds passed before the barber's sun-bronzed cheery face appeared round the door. Seeing Gunn, he pales and the smile vanishes. 'Sure didn't reckon on seeing you here again,' he muttered, nervously.

Gunn's face was set and grim. 'Ain't here for a shave this time,' he told the man. 'Don't care much for the way your part-time help carry out their chores.'

The barber looked even more nervous. 'Then what can I do for you, Mister Gunn?'

'Want some information,' Gunn snapped back. 'The Shobrook boys. Where do I find them?'

The barber licked his lips, shaking his head slightly. 'Look, I don't want to get mixed up in no trouble,' he bleated.

Gunn was in no mood to pussyfoot around. His right-hand Colt leapt from its holster into his palm. His finger caressed the trigger gently. 'I didn't say please,' he murmured suggestively. 'And there won't be any trouble. Not for you anyway. Provided, of course, I get the service I came in here for.'

The barber looked down the business end of the Colt and then up into Gunn's cold, ice-blue eyes. Both looked equally dangerous. He decided to talk. 'None of the Shobrook boys been in town much lately,' he volunteered. 'People bin joking about maybe they gone on the wagon.'

'So where's their spread?'

The barber jerked his head out towards the back of the shop. 'East. 'Bout four miles or so, along the old dry creek run. You can't miss it.'

'Big spread? How many hands?' Gunn wanted to

know. He needed to have a good picture of what he might be up against.

The barber shook his head. 'Not so big. Ain't enough water to carry too many cattle. Besides old man Shobrook and the three boys, they only have two hired hands.'

Gunn nodded thoughtfully, digesting the information he had received. Assuming the hired hands would back up their employers with guns, that set six men against him. Not good odds, by anyone's standards. It looked nigh-on impossible to consider riding out alone – yet there was absolutely no one he could turn to for help of any kind. His eyes roved to the barber shop window and out across the street. They set upon the sheriff's office, with the jail tucked out of sight behind it. Gunn's mind turned over possibilities in a neat, logical manner.

Eventually, there was only one answer. Somehow, he had to bust John Cunningham out of jail. The man had nothing to lose, for his life was on a two-day mortgage anyway. Together, they stood a chance of taking on the Shobrook family and forcing the truth out of any one of them. Alone, Cunningham would die and Gunn could do nothing to help him.

His mind made up, Gunn turned back to the little barber. His eyes narrowed threateningly. Slowly, he cocked the hammer of the Colt and aimed it between the man's eyes. 'If you know what's good for you, you'll keep this little visit strictly to yourself,' he hissed with quiet menace. 'You know what I mean?'

The barber nodded energetically. 'Sure, Mister Gunn. I ain't seen you since the shooting,' he gushed, over-enthusiastically.

'Right. And don't you forget it,' Gunn reminded him, slowly slipping the hammer of his Colt back into position. 'You breathe a word and you're a dead man.'

He took a last, careful look at the man's terrified expression and felt satisfied that his threats had achieved their intention. The barber would keep his mouth shut – at least for a while. With a last angry glare, he slipped the ivory handled Colt back into its holster and swivelled on one heel. He walked out of the shop without a word, stepping lightly out on to the boardwalk and through the nearest gap between the wooden shop-fronts and away from the main street. Skirting along behind the buildings, he walked until he was level with the sheriff's office again and checked the street. Things were still quiet. Satisfied that no one was around, Gunn stepped smartly out into the street again, crossed it and unhitched his horse from the rail. He swung himself into the saddle in one smooth movement and was galloping out of town in a matter of seconds.

He headed back towards the Circle 8. He would need a good spare horse and some extra firepower, if his plan was to stand any chance of succeeding. As he neared the ranch house, Lydia Cunningham rushed out to greet him.

'Any news, James?' she called out to him as he dismounted.

Gunn forced a hopeful smile on his face. He did not want Lydia to know what he was planning. There was a strong possibility that her husband would be gunned down in the escape bid. Right now, what Lydia Cunningham needed was hope, and some rest. 'It's OK, everything's going to be fine,' he lied, walking across to her. 'I fixed everything up with Sheriff Baines. There's just a few legal papers he has to draw up, and then John will be released. I'm taking a horse back for him in an hour or so.'

Lydia's face beamed with happiness and relief. She ran across the last few yards between them and flung her arms around his neck. Squeezing him tightly, she burst into tears of happiness. 'God, James, thank goodness you got back in time.'

Gunn gently disengaged her hands from around his neck and slipped a comforting arm around her slim waist. Still wearing his forced smile, he looked down at her and winked. 'Think I must be getting a mite soft in the head, getting John out of jail when he's got a beautiful woman like you going free,' he joked with her. Gently he propelled her towards the house. 'If it's all right with you, Lydia, I could sure use a cup of coffee and a bite to eat.'

Chapter Twelve

Lydia Cunningham's initial feelings of joy and relief had already begun to fade before she watched Gunn start saddling up the two Mexican stallions. Over the meal, Gunn had found it virtually impossible to keep up the pretence that all was well. Lydia was a sensitive and intelligent woman – well able to probe beyond the vague sense of unease which permeated the ranch house. The black stallions were the final clue.

Even then, Lydia didn't want to ask directly. She preferred to at least attempt to continue believing in the lie. 'Why the stallions, James?'

He tried to bluff it out, save Lydia from realising that he was taking the fastest horses he could think of, knowing that he and John Cunningham were going to need every bit of advantage they could muster. 'Thought it would be a nice surprise for him,' he lied, forcing the carefree smile again. 'A sort of coming out present.'

Lydia knew then. 'You mean a breaking-out present, don't you James?' she said quietly.

Gunn looked at her with a new surge of admiration. She was a brave woman, Lydia Cunningham. Even now, facing the harsh truth, she was calm and rational. It was pointless trying to mislead her any further. The smile faded from Gunn's face. 'Yes,' he answered, simply and softly. 'It's the only chance he's got, Lydia.'

She nodded understandingly. 'You're a good man, James. A good friend for a man to have. I know you're risking your life to save John.'

He made no answer. Swinging himself up into the

saddle, he took a last-minute check on his equipment. Spare guns, food and water for two, a couple of rifles and plenty of ammunition. They might need every last bullet to keep their freedom. Ready to leave, he looked down at Lydia again. 'I'll bring him back to you, I promise,' he vowed in a soft, yet confident voice.

Lydia Cunningham compressed her lips, nodding gently. 'If you have to go on the run, James, tell John I'll sell up here and meet him in Green Valley, Oregon. We have friends there. He can hide out and be safe.'

'There'll be no need,' Gunn assured her. 'We'll be back in two days at the most – with John's innocence established.'

He spurred his stallion, leading the spare behind him. Lydia Cunningham watched him fade into the distance, hoping against hope that she was not wrong in believing his last words. When the two horses were only a speck on the horizon, she turned and walked back towards the house. Only then did her control break again. Throwing herself upon the bed, she began the passionate sobbing which would carry on all through the coming night.

Gunn waited outside the town limits for sundown. As the light faded, and the sinking sun threw chocolate-brown shadows between the buildings, he urged his horse forward again. If he had figured it right, Sheriff Baines would just be about ready to start his last patrol around the town before night fell. That would leave just his deputy to deal with. Even so, Gunn fully realised the difficulties of the task he had set himself. Somehow, he had to break Cunningham out of jail without a killing – preferably without any shooting at all. It was the only way. If anyone died in the process, Cunningham's cause would be lost for ever, and in all probability, they would both hang from the same gallows.

He trotted the horses around the back of the jail first, on an initial scouting expedition. As he had thought, there was little hope in that quarter. The single window into the jail interior was too high and too small for a

106

man to crawl through, even if the heavy steel bars could be torn out. Gunn thought about trying to contact Cunningham and warn him of his intentions, then decided against it. The element of surprise and a certain degree of confusion would help his plans rather than hinder them. Quietly, he led the horses back into the main street and took a careful look around.

The door of the sheriff's office opened. Gunn threw himself back into the shadows, stroking the horses gently to keep them quiet. Sheriff Baines stepped out on to the boardwalk, lazily casting his gaze from side to side. He leaned against a post and casually rolled a cigarette. It was a quiet evening. He wasn't expecting any trouble. There was time for a smoke before he made his rounds.

Gunn waited. He was in no great hurry, either. As the minutes passed, his mind continued to chew over the chances and the possibilities open to him. With a sudden flash of clarity, he realised that his original plan was slightly faulty. If he allowed Baines to set out on his rounds, there was the strong possibility that he would carry the cell keys on his person. Even if Gunn got the deputy cold, he would not be able to set Cunningham free, even under threat of death. There was another factor to consider as well; while Baines was close and free, he was in a strong position to round up a quick posse and give chase. Gunn and Cunningham stood a better chance if they could get away with a bit of a start.

With this realisation dawning on him, Gunn speedily reconsidered and formulated a new plan. To put it into action, he stooped to the ground, scrabbling in the dust with his fingers. He found what he was looking for; a small, rounded pebble, about the size of a hen's egg. Standing up again, he quietly slipped his black leather bullwhip from its holster on his horse's saddle. Carefully, he knotted the end around the pebble, pulling it tight.

With a bold, purposeful step, he strode out from the

shadows and headed down the street towards the sheriff's office. His plan depended upon his getting as close to Baines as possible before the man thought anything might be amiss. Any shifty action would arouse the man's suspicion.

The ploy worked. Baines caught a vague glimpse of a man strolling towards him out of the corner of his eye, but the sight barely registered. Not until it was too late! As Gunn approached him, Baines glanced up, casually. Recognising Gunn by his height and colouring, Baines sensed trouble instinctively. 'Gunn?' he hissed in the same second that his hand clawed towards his holster.

His fingers never closed around the butt. Poised and ready as he moved, Gunn lashed out with the whip, sending the missile bound to its tip flying straight and true. The pebble cracked neatly against Baines' temple, stunning him instantly. Without a sound, the sheriff crumpled to the ground in a senseless heap.

In one smooth bound, Gunn leapt over his body and opened the door. His right-hand Colt was firmly in his grasp as he jumped through the portal.

'Freeze, or you're a dead man,' he barked at the deputy, seated at the desk.

The deputy looked up, his face draining of colour with the shock and surprise. Slowly and deliberately, he moved his hands away from his side and high into the air before placing them softly, palms down upon the top of the desk. It was no time to act brave. A man could get good and dead that way.

Gunn breathed a sigh of relief at the deputy's reaction. Things were going more smoothly than he had dared to hope. The Colt in his hand jerked slightly. 'Stand up.'

The deputy pushed his chair back and stood, making sure that he was well clear of the desk so that Gunn could see every movement clearly.

'Come over here,' Gunn commanded. The deputy obeyed without the slightest attempt at protest. 'Turn round.'

As the deputy presented his back, Gunn slipped his single Army Colt from its holster and tossed it into the corner. He jabbed the muzzle of his own Colt in the man's ribs and gave out his immediate orders. 'Drag Sheriff Baines in here – as quietly as possible. Don't forget this gun won't be far away from your backbone.'

He prodded the man towards the door. Opening it, the deputy glanced nervously out into the quiet, darkened street before stooping down to grab the unconscious sheriff by his feet and drag him in through the doorway.

'Get the keys,' Gunn snapped.

The deputy bent over his superior and rummaged in his pockets, finally pulling out a heavy bunch of keys on a small chain link.

'Get Cunningham,' Gunn told him curtly. Silently, the deputy slunk off towards the cells.

On the floor, Baines groaned and moved his head. Swiftly, Gunn bent down and removed his gun, throwing it to join that of his deputy. As Baines opened his eyes, Gunn waved the muzzle of his Colt in the man's face. 'Not so much as a whisper, sheriff,' he warned.

Baines glared up with undisguised hatred. Despite the warning, he could not keep quiet. 'My God, I'll see you swing for this, Gunn,' he hissed. 'I'll hunt you down, I swear it.'

Gunn smiled thinly. 'You won't need to, sheriff. Just as soon as I establish Cunningham's innocence, we'll both be back. You can do what you think fit, then.'

'You're a fool, Gunn,' sheriff Baines spat at him contemptuously. 'You ain't got a snowball's chance in hell.'

'I don't melt that easy,' Gunn countered. 'Besides, whatever you really think, sheriff, we've got right on our side. And I guess that still counts for something, even in this town.'

He looked up as the deputy walked back into the room with Cunningham close on his heels.

'Jim,' Cunningham burst out. 'What's happening?'

'We're getting out of here, John,' Gunn told him

109

calmly. Then, turning back to the deputy: 'You got some rope around here?'

The man nodded towards a closet in the wall. 'In there.'

'Get it, John,' Gunn said quietly. As Cunningham fetched the rope, he jerked his Colt under the deputy's nose. 'Sit down on the floor, next to the sheriff. Put your hands behind your back.'

Wordlessly, the man obeyed. Cunningham returned with the rope, holding it out. Gunn passed him his Colt, taking the rope. Bending down, he quickly and expertly bound the two men together, lashed their feet and wrapped the end of the rope around the legs of the heavy desk. Finishing that chore, he removed the black bandana from around his neck and fashioned an efficient gag for Baines. Doing the same for his deputy with a piece of rag the sheriff had been using to clean his rifles, Gunn stood up again, satisfied that both men were out of action for some time to come.

'That should give us a good headstart,' he muttered to Cunningham. 'Guess it's time to ride.'

Cunningham nodded. 'Damn right,' he breathed, fervently.

The two men moved to the door. Gunn inched it open, peering out into the street. There was no one in sight. 'Let's go,' he hissed, throwing the door fully open and stepping briskly out on to the boardwalk. Once outside, they made a quick dash towards the horses.

Across the street, the saloon doors swung open and a man walked out into the street. He stopped dead, staring out across the dark street at the two fleeing figures. Somehow, recognition dawned on him. 'It's Cunningham,' he screamed out in a loud voice. 'He's breaking outta jail.'

Gunn saw the man's hand move towards the gun at his side. He dropped quickly to his knees, his own Colt at the ready, swearing under his breath. He had wanted to avoid any shooting, get out of town quietly and quickly, without the alarm being raised. Now, that hope was gone.

The man drew his gun. In the darkness, Gunn saw the small tongues of flame spit from the muzzle as the Colt spewed death across the street.

Taking careful aim, Gunn fired three shots in quick succession. His aim was true, and served its purpose. The man threw himself backwards into the safety of the saloon as each slug chewed up dust only inches from his feet. Gunn slammed off two more shots into the saloon door before scrambling to his feet again and completing the dash to the horses. Cunningham was already mounted. In the panic, he had not even noticed that he was astride one of the black stallions he had coveted for so long.

Gunn swung himself up into the saddle and jabbed his heels hard into the animal's flank, pulling hard on the reins to wheel the horse around. Behind them, men were starting to pour out of the saloon, and a steady crack of gunshots was building up into a fusillade. With lead whining through the air all around them, Gunn and Cunningham galloped out of town, out into the temporary safety of the desert night.

There was no real attempt at pursuit. There really wasn't much point. A few of the townsfolk got as far as mounting up and riding to the outskirts of town, but the blackness of the open desert had swallowed their prey up completely. Cursing and making dire threats, the would-be pursuers saw the futility of their task and drifted back into town, to wait until morning. There was no wind, so the trail should still be fresh and clear at sun-up.

Gunn led the two horses at a blistering pace for several miles. Only when he felt that they were clear of town and with no pursuers did he allow his mount to slow to a more comfortable pace. Cunningham eased into position alongside him. 'Where we headed, Jim?'

'Tonight, we'll camp out in the desert,' Gunn told him. 'First light tomorrow, we're heading for the Shobrook ranch. I got a strong feeling that's where the answers lie.'

'Whatever you say, Jim,' Cunningham murmured. 'And thanks.'

Chapter Thirteen

They slept rough, on bare bedrolls, with only the shelter of a few clumps of sagebrush against the cool night air. At sun-up, the two men contented themselves with a few sips of water and a couple of hard-tack biscuits for breakfast, not wanting to run the attendant risks of lighting a fire. They were fugitives, condemned to exist below the normal living standards of men for as long as they remained outside the law.

Hopefully, that would not be for long, Gunn promised himself. He was more and more convinced now that the key to the whole business lay in her personal feud with the Shobrook brothers. The only real trouble which remained was in forcing out the right answers . . . in front of the right witnesses.

Gunn re-checked his Colts and rifle before saddling up. He glanced back across the desert in the vague direction of Sagebrush Flats, feeling a sense of unease at seeing the plain mark of their tracks the previous night. Gunn knew for sure that Baines would already have been up and about, rounding up a posse to come in chase. They would have a clear path to follow. There wasn't much time. For a moment, Gunn considered the possibility of attempting to lay a false trail, before rejecting it as unworkable. Out here in the desert, it was no easy task, and would take up far too much valuable time. There was, however, one small thing he could do to at least confuse the issue for any pursuers.

Acting accordingly, Gunn slipped his Bowie knife from his belt and cut off two stout branches of sagebrush. Quickly tying them to the long black tails of the two stallions, he adjusted them until the leafy fronds just brushed the desert floor. An old Indian trick, it would serve to stir up dust behind the passage of the horses, if not actually removing traces of their passing, then at least obscuring it to a certain extent. At best, the ploy would only slow down their pursuers – but any time gained was valuable. As a secondary precaution, Gunn and Cunningham rode away from their camp site in opposite directions, making a large circular detour before heading in the same direction. Even then, the two riders kept a good fifty yards between them, frequently zig-zagging their mounts in diversions which did not waste too much time.

In terms of normal riding time, it should have been just over an hour to the Shobrook ranch. With their diversionary tactics, it took nearly two, but Gunn felt sure that Baines and his posse would lose a further two hours sorting out the muddled trail. If nothing else, it doubled their safety margin.

The rugged bed of the dried-up creek was a perfect signpost, just as the barber had told him. Gunn urged his horse in towards it as they neared the Shobrook spread, signalling Cunningham to do the same. For the last half mile, the two riders came together again and guided their mounts gently down the shallow sides of the creek into the gulley. It wasn't deep, but it would at least give them a certain amount of cover in the flat, featureless desert.

Stopping to remove the remnants of sagebrush from the tails of the stallions, Gunn looked up at his companion with a grim smile. 'It won't be long now, John.'

Cunningham nodded wordlessly. He could feel the rising tension inside himself. Before the morning was out, he would know his fate. There were three possibilities; he would be a free man, having proved his innocence, he would be a fugitive for all time . . . or he would be dead. Even with the most wildly optimistic nature, the latter seemed the most likely.

'Ready then?' Gunn asked quietly, sensing his friend's mood.

Cunningham nodded again. 'Ready,' he affirmed, gently spurring his horse into movement. The two riders trotted slowly along the rocky bottom of the old creek. It had been dry for many years now, since the spring which had fed it petered out. Today, its dry bed might flow again – but with blood instead of water.

They got to within three hundred yards of the quiet ranch-house. Suddenly, a rifle bullet whined off the top of the gulley, passing over their heads. Both Gunn and Cunningham threw themselves down out of the saddles as a weak voice called out from the house. 'That was just a warning, who ever you are out there. Don't reckon to trust anybody who sneaks up like a thief. Better identify yourself, gents. And your business.'

Cunningham turned to Gunn. 'That's old man Shobrook's voice,' he whispered. 'He always was a wary old buzzard.'

'Early riser, too,' Gunn observed dryly. Inching forwards on his belly, he pushed himself up the side of the creek to get a clear view of the house. A second slug chewed up a few inches from his face as he neared the top. Pressing himself into the ground, he slithered back again. 'Guess they can see more of us than we can see of them,' he muttered.

Cunningham grunted. 'More or less stalemate, the way things are,' he observed. 'Guess I could at least try talking to him.' He crawled a little way up the slope and cupped his hands around his mouth. 'Shobrook? This is John Cunningham. Ain't got no call to get into a shooting match with you, but I sure got business with your boys.'

The answer came back quickly. It was emphatic: 'You got business with any one of the Shobrooks, and you got business with all of us.'

'You got Gunn there with you, Cunningham?' a younger voice called out.

'That's Jess,' Cunningham said quietly, recognising

115

the voice. It was swiftly followed by two others. 'Best give yourself up, Cunningham. We only want Gunn.' Then: 'Yeah, this is family, Cunningham. Turn Gunn over to us and we could maybe swing something with the sheriff.'

'Wesley and Brendan,' Cunningham said, identifying the other two brothers. 'Looks like we just stirred ourselves up the whole damned hornet's nest.'

As if to give backing to his words, a sustained volley of gunfire cracked out from the house. Behind Gunn and Cunningham, a dozen slugs chewed into the far side of the gulley, spewing up dust and small stones.

'Hornets without a sting, though,' Gunn observed, noting where the bullets had struck. 'Looks like they can't get a clear line of fire so long as we stay put. They can only fire over our heads.'

'Like I said, it's a stalemate,' Cunningham reiterated. 'They can't get at us and we can't get at them. All we can do is hole up here until the posse catch up with us.'

'Maybe,' Gunn muttered distantly. He was racking his brains, trying to figure out an angle. Nothing sprang immediately to mind. Fifteen or twenty minutes passed, with no action from the Shobrook house. They too were considering the problem.

At last, Jess' voice barked out again. 'Well, Cunningham? Want to make some sort of a deal?'

Gunn prodded his friend in the ribs. 'Talk to him,' he hissed. 'Keep him busy, see what he has to say. I'm going to sneak further up the gulley to see if I can get a better view.'

Cunningham nodded, understanding. He lifted his head and shouted back towards the house. 'What sort of deal you got in mind, Jess?'

Gunn didn't bother to try and listen to the shouted conversation as he crawled along the gulley on his belly. Right that minute, he was not at all interested in whatever deals Jess Shobrook was willing to make. His sole interest was in finding a way out of the dilemma he and Cunningham had blundered into.

116

The going got rougher up the creek bed. The bottom was thick with loose shale, and the rocks were not as smooth and rounded as they had been further down the run. Here, closer to the original source, the broken rocks and stones had been split off from larger boulders, and had not had their rough edges rounded off by the constant flow of water over the years. Sharp edges of flint and crystalline basalt tore and scratched at his clothing and skin, drawing off a small sacrifice of blood from dozens of grazes.

Gunn made about another thirty yards before he came to a flat bowl. It was the end of the line. He could go no further without breaking cover and placing himself in the direct line of fire from six rifles. Carefully, he edged up the slope and took a quick look over the top towards the house.

He was just in time to see a running figure leave the back entrance of the house and scuttle across to the stone well built in the rear courtyard. Obviously, the Shobrooks had made much the same decision – to investigate the possibilities of an attack from the rear.

Though it was only a glimpse, Gunn saw enough of the running man to note that he was young, and definitely not one of the Shobrook brothers. One of the hired hands, then. That caused problems. Gunn had no wish to kill an innocent employee, helplessly caught up in something which was not his problem, or part of his job.

Gunn continued to stare at the well, where the man had gone to ground. Reaching behind him, he gripped his rifle by the barrel and hauled it up towards him, crooking the butt firmly under his arm and caressing the trigger. Something told him that the hand would make a second dash, from the well to a nearby cattle trough, some twelve feet away.

He was right. Crouched, the man broke cover as Gunn watched, sprinting across the intervening space with the speed of a man knowing his life was at risk. He wasn't quite quick enough to evade Gunn's lightning aim.

Snapping the rifle up into position, Gunn squinted along the sights and moved the rifle in a smooth line along the man's path. Praying that his aim was true, Gunn gently squeezed the trigger.

The rifle bullet sped accurately to its target. The running man threw his own Springfield into the air as the slug embedded itself deep in the hard muscle of his arm, a few inches down from the shoulder. His legs buckled under him from the impact and the sudden pain, but sheer desperation and the need for survival enabled him to run the last few feet to safety. He threw himself down behind the horse trough.

Gunn lay the rifle down and called out. 'You there. Get back to the house and have someone tend your wound. I don't want to kill you. This is not your fight.'

There was silence. The man was not convinced. Gunn tried again. 'That slug was intended for your right shoulder. I could have killed you. All I've done is put your gun-arm out of action. Now do what I say and get back to the house.'

A few moments passed. Then, gradually, the injured man pushed himself out from behind the trough, squirming on the ground with his legs and good arm so as not to present too much of a target. Only when he had covered three or four feet in this way did he accept the fact that he was not going to be shot down. With obvious relief, he dragged himself to his feet and loped back to the house, his left hand pressed over his wounded arm.

Gunn retrieved his rifle, slid back down the slope and began to crawl back towards Cunningham. He was satisfied that the Shobrooks would not attempt to sneak a man out of the back again for a good while.

'Any luck?' Cunningham wanted to know as Gunn returned.

Gunn shrugged. 'One of the hands is out of the fight,' he replied, simply.

Cunningham grunted. 'Cuts the odds, I guess. D'ya hear what Jess Shobrook had to say for himself?'

118

Gunn shook his head. 'I was busy.'

'Boy, them Shobrooks want you real bad,' Cunningham went on. 'I practically got offered a free pardon from the State Governor if I'd turn you over.'

Gunn forced a smile. 'Thinking about it?'

Cunningham returned the humour. 'Best offer I've had so far today,' he quipped. 'You had any bright ideas yet?'

Gunn sucked at his bottom lip pensively. There was one scheme he had been chewing over on his way back down the gulley. 'Depends how desperate we get,' he murmured, guardedly.

He broke off to stare down the dry creek in the direction they had come. 'Reckon Baines and his posse should just about be sorting out our trail,' he observed, rather distantly.

'So?' Cunningham wanted to know.

'Just wondered if he might be able to use a little help . . . get things speeded up,' Gunn muttered.

Cunningham looked at him aghast. 'You gone plumb loco, Jim?' We got enough trouble, without Sheriff Baines on us as well.'

'Maybe,' Gunn said quietly. 'Maybe not.'

Cunningham peered intently into his friend's eyes. 'What's on your mind, Jim?'

Gunn appeared to be thinking for a few moments longer. Finally, he nodded, as if to himself. 'Yep, I guess we really are pretty desperate at that.'

Without explaining, he slithered across to his horse, safely tucked away behind one of the few stunted trees which fringed the dry creek's lip. He gathered the reins in with one hand, leading the animal down to the bottom of the gulley-bed and pointing it back towards Sagebrush Fats.

'What are you doing, Jim?' Cunningham whispered again.

Gunn pulled a wry face. 'Times like this, a man needs the law on his side,' he said quietly. 'I figure if we could get this far without being spotted from the house, I can

119

bring Baines and a couple of his men back up the same way. It's the only real chance we got, the way I see it.'

Cunningham shook his head in confusion. 'You've lost me, Jim.'

'Just stay put. Keep your head down,' Gunn shot back. 'With luck, nobody'll even know I've gone. Even if they do figure it out, there's no real chance of them rushing you without being picked off like flies.'

Cunningham watched Gunn lead the horse away back down the creek-bed, his hand tight on the reins so that the creature's head was pulled down out of sight. He still didn't understand, but he breathed a message of good luck under his breath anyway. Gunn would need it. He was going back to meet an irate lawman who was quite likely to shoot first and ask questions afterwards. And Baines was no slouch when it came to using a hand gun.

Gunn walked the black stallion for a half mile before he felt it safe to mount up. The creek had bent round in a virtual half-circle, and there seemed little chance of being spotted from the Shobrook ranch. Slipping neatly up into the saddle, Gunn guided the animal carefully through the shale and loose rocks.

Half an hour later, he spurred the horse in the flanks and rode it up the sloping side of the gulley on to the flat scrubland again. Now he could make up a bit of time. He urged the stallion into a fast gallop, towards a swirling patch of dust in the distance. As he rode, Gunn slipped his rifle from its saddle-holster and held it high above his head, horizontally. Devoid of a truce-flag, it was the best he could do to give Baines an advance signal that he was coming in quietly.

The posse was eight strong. Baines obviously had a healthy respect for Gunn's firepower. Luckily, he recognised Gunn's gesture for what it was, and was sufficiently in control of his men to prevent them from getting trigger happy as their quarry approached them so unexpectedly. Reining in his mount with one hand, Gunn was able to ride right up to the group without a shot being fired – although he did come to a stop facing the business end of at least six drawn Colts.

'Throw down the rifle, Gunn. Keep your hands high,' Baines barked at once.

Gunn smiled, tossing the rifle across to the sheriff, who caught it neatly with one hand.

Baines stared at him in wonderment for a while. Finally he spoke, and there was obvious bewilderment in his voice. 'I swear you're crazy, Gunn, Crazier'n a mule in March.'

'Come to make you a little proposition, sheriff,' Gunn said, a sight more brightly than he really felt. He was sure that Baines would have a real stinker of a headache from the blow which had knocked him cold the previous night. He was unlikely to be in good humour, or predisposed towards friendliness for a man who had shown him up in front of the entire town.

'Proposition?' Baines' eyes nearly popped out of his head. 'What in tarnation are you talking about? You ride up to a fully-armed posse and start talking about making deals?'

'All right, I'll spell it out for you,' Gunn said, suddenly in dead earnest. He might not have much time to play with, now that the sheriff's initial shock and surprise was starting to wear off. 'This is the pitch – straight and simple. I know that Cunningham is innocent, and I know that the Shobrook brothers are responsible for the killing of old Elmer. What's more, I think I can prove it to you. All I'm asking is just half an hour of your time. After that, you can take me and Cunningham straight back to jail.' He paused for a few seconds, letting the message sink in. 'Well, how about it?'

Sheriff Baines creased his brow with thought. He was plainly uncertain of himself and just what he was being asked to get into. Finally, he heaved a sigh of exasperation. 'Gunn, I guess I must be getting a mite crazy myself, but I can't help feeling you're handing me a straight pitch. Dammit, I can't for the life of me see why else you should come riding up here to give yourself up without a fight.'

'That's what I hoped, sheriff,' Gunn told him. 'It was the best chance we had.'

'Well, what you got in mind?' Baines asked flatly.

Gunn explained his plan, in all its simplicity. Baines and his deputy would ride with him back up the gulley, leaving the rest of the posse behind. They would get back within earshot of the Shobrook ranch without being seen, and with luck, Baines would hear one of the brothers make a full confession – without any pressure being brought to bear.

Baines looked sceptical. 'You want me to leave my posse and ride along with you so that Cunningham can pick us off with a rifle?'

Gunn shook his head. 'Trust me, Baines,' he insisted. 'You can ride right behind me, with a rifle stuck in my back.'

Baines thought about it for a few more seconds, finally having to admit that Gunn's plan seemed sound. 'OK,' he snapped at last. 'We'll play it your way. Take off your gunbelt – nice and easy.'

Gunn slipped off his twin Colts and threw the complete rig across to Baines. Wheeling his horse, he pointed it back towards the creek. 'Now we ride real slow, real quiet, and with our heads kept well down,' he said.

Baines' voice followed over his shoulder. 'Whatever you say, Gunn. For half an hour, no longer.'

Slowly, the small group detached from the main party and headed back down the gully to the Shobrook ranch. As they neared Cunningham, he spread his hands way out wide to show there were no tricks up his sleeve. At gunpoint, Baines disarmed him.

'Well, I've kept my word sheriff. Now will you trust me?' Gunn asked in a whisper.

The sheriff nodded. 'I'll keep mine,' he promised.

Gunn nodded grimly. Now came the most dangerous part of his plan. He was about to lay his life on the line. He crawled close to John Cunningham, to rehearse him in his role in the little charade to come. Cunningham listened intently, finally nodding gravely.

Gunn turned back to Baines. 'I'll need my rifle, sheriff. One shot up the spout,' he said.

Baines looked at him dubiously for a moment. 'No tricks, now,' he warned.

'No tricks.' Gunn watched as the sheriff cracked open his Springfield and pumped out five of its shells. He handed it over gingerly.

'Right. Here goes,' Gunn muttered, and began scrambling up the sloping side of the gully. Nearing the top, he scrambled to his feet and stood, fully exposed to the ranch house for just long enough to sqeeze off the single shot.

The air echoed with the crash of half a dozen shots in return. With a scream of pain, Gunn fell backwards into the gulley, the rifle dropping from his hands.

He fell heavily, rolling back down the slope to the bottom. Baines and Cunningham looked down at him in alarm.

'Looks like his little plan didn't work,' Baines observed laconically.

His face was a picture of confusion as the 'corpse' at the bottom of the creek rolled over, sat up, and grinned with relief. Gunn's timing had been perfect. It had been a gamble, but one which had paid off. He had counted on showing himself for just long enough for several of the Shobrook clan to take aim. Although, in reality, he had thrown himself down the merest fraction of a second before the first trigger was pulled, those in the house could only assume that it was some-one else's shot which had got him. As far as they were concerned, Gunn was hit – and either dead or badly wounded. Now it was time for Cunningham to play his part. He bided his time, letting the Shobrooks get them-selves into a self-congratulatory mood.

Finally, he cupped his hands around his mouth and shouted. 'Jess, it's Cunningham.'

Jess Shobrook's voice drifted back. He sounded jubi-lant. 'Yeah, Cunningham, what do you want?'

'Gunn's hit,' Cunningham answered. 'He's wounded

123

real bad. You were talking about some kind of deal earlier. Things look a mite different now. I might be interested. What you offering?'

A nasty laugh came back from the house. 'No dice, Cunningham. You had your chance. It's just a matter of time now until we pick you off too.'

Cunningham was playing his part well. He injected a tone of cringing fear into his voice. 'Look, I told you – Gunn's dying. It was him you wanted to get even with, wasn't it? You can let me off the hook now – you don't have to kill me.'

Again, Jess Shobrook's voice came back with a vicious edge to it. 'Sorry, Cunningham, but I gotta kill you, sure as hell. The way I see it, you and Gunn musta figured out it was me who framed you, otherwise you wouldn't have come riding out here. Don't aim to swing for murder, Cunningham, and I figure you know too much to live.'

Gunn's face was jubilant as he turned to sheriff Baines. 'Good enough for you, sheriff?'

Baines nodded grimly. 'Guess I've heard enough,' he muttered. He tossed Gunn's gunbelt across to him and turned towards the ranch house. 'Jess?' he called out. 'This is Sheriff Baines. Reckon we got something to talk about back at the jailhouse.'

There was a shocked, silence. Baines started to stand up. Gunn leapt up behind him, pulling him down. 'Are you crazy?' That trigger-happy kid ain't going to let you take him in. He'll gun you down as soon as you show your face.'

Baines tried to pull away. 'I'm the law, Gunn,' he muttered grimly. 'People gotta respect that.'

'People like Jess Shobrook only respect the Colt,' Gunn said. 'And it's my bet he and his brothers are getting ready to face up to that right this minute.'

Baines didn't understand. 'What do you mean, Gunn?'

Gunn gestured further up the gulley. 'My bet is that they'll make a break out of the back of the house any minute now,' he said quietly. 'They'll expect to take us by surprise and shoot it out right now.'

As he spoke, Gunn drew his right-hand Colt and pressed himself into the side of the gulley. 'If you'll take my advice, you'll do the same, sheriff,' he warned.

Baines hesitated – for just too long. From the flat bowl at the end of the gully, the three Shobrook brothers appeared, standing in a line. Each held a Colt in either hand.

Six tongues of flame belched simultaneously. A hail of flying lead whined along both sides of the gully as the Shobrooks fired at random.

Baines gave a grunt of pain as a slug chewed into his upper chest, he slumped back, out of the line of fire, leaving a clear path for Wesley Shobrook to pump a .45 slug into the middle of his deputy's belly.

Cunningham's Walker-Colt barked once. Wesley seemed to double up, his knees slowly buckling under him. Then, slowly, he toppled forward with a neat hole drilled through his heart. He lay face-down in the dust.

Gunn pushed himself out from the side of the gulley, fanning his Colt with the speed of a striking rattler. The hammer flashed five times, discharging what was left in the chamber. Two of the bullets took Brendan Shobrook in the thigh and groin. He shrieked in agony and collapsed, to writhe horribly for a few seconds, finally to lay still.

Jess Shobrook saw his second brother fall and threw himself backwards, into the cover of the shallow dust-bowl. A few seconds passed as he hastily reloaded his guns.

'Gunn, you bastard,' he screamed out after a while. 'Just you and me, Gunn, what do you say?'

Gunn slipped his other Colt from its holster, spinning the chamber experimentally. 'Yeah. Just you and me, Shobrook,' he called back.

Cunningham looked up at him in alarm. 'Careful, Jim.'

Gunn's face was set in a grim mask. He stood up slowly, the Colt ready in his hand, dangling by his side.

His keen eyes stared straight up the gulley, watching, waiting.

Jess Shobrook jumped to his feet, his Colt blazing fire. Gunn jumped to one side as slugs churned up dust at his immediate rear. His hand flashed upwards, the heavy Cavalry Colt bucking gently in his hand as he fired on the rise.

Jess Shobrook's body stiffened as the slug ripped into his left shoulder. The arm flopped uselessly by his side, but he remained standing. His right hand brought his Colt up to fire again. He staggered forward.

Gunn squeezed off another shot. It took Jess full in the chest, the impact stopping him dead in his tracks. Miraculously, Jess still remained on his feet. He seemed unstoppable.

Gunn held his fire, convinced that the youngster was about to drop. He wasn't. With something like super-human effort, Jess made another lurch forward, and fired off another shot which sang past Gunn's ear.

Gunn dropped instinctively to his knees, swinging up his Colt and firing for the third time. Jess Shobrook's face exploded in a crimson horror mask as the heavy bullet smashed through the centre of his nose, smashing bone and flesh on its destructive path deep into his brain.

For a half second longer, his dead body remained upright. Then, pushed back off balance by the impetus of the slug, it collapsed sideways, to sprawl across the corpses of his two brothers.

Gunn sighed heavily, lowering his Colt. He turned to look down at Sheriff Baines and his wound. It was not as serious at it looked. There was a lot of blood, but the bullet had gone in well above the heart, and several inches clear of the lungs. Baines would be all right.

The sheriff looked up at Gunn through watery eyes and managed a brave, slightly apologetic, smile. 'Sorry I didn't believe you earlier, Gunn,' he murmured sheepishly.

Gunn grunted, with a trace of bitterness. 'Yeah. So am I,' he said, flatly. He was in no mood to accept apologies gracefully, or even attempt politeness.

Too many people had died for that.

MEWS BESTSELLERS
